DUBLIN'S
STRANGEST
TALES

For your reading pleasure

DUBLIN'S
STRANGEST
TALES

EXTRAORDINARY
BUT TRUE STORIES

A VERY CURIOUS HISTORY

MICHAEL BARRY & PATRICK SAMMON

PORTICO

First published in the United Kingdom in 2013 by
Portico Books
10 Southcombe Street
London
W14 0RA

An imprint of Anova Books Company Ltd

ISBN 9781907554926

A CIP catalogue record for this book is available from the British Library.

10 9 8 7 6 5 4 3 2 1

Printed and bound by Toppan Leefung Printing Limited, China

This book can be ordered direct from the publisher at
www.anovabooks.com

CONTENTS

INTRODUCTION:
DUBLIN – REDOUBT
OF THE STRANGE

When Paddy and I first sat down to write *Dublin's Strangest Tales*, it did not take us long to realise that we would have a wealth of events to choose from. The piquant, the strange, the odd – all have sparked the receptor cells in our brains – we have been collecting, enjoying and talking about these topics for years.

And what better place than Dublin? It is a veritable redoubt of the strange and the city seems to have worked hard at this over the centuries. Our tales cover the many centuries of Dublin's existence, from the Vikings through to the dog (or should that be cat?) days of the little-lamented Celtic Tiger.

This is a Dublin many may not have encountered. Some of these stories are dark, with twists (some subtle, others more blunt) that you might not have associated with the city. We hope you will *bain taitneamh as* (get enjoyment from it). It all reflects the quirky and occasionally volcanic history of Dublin down the ages.

Some British or American readers, fed on a diet of blather about blarney, leprechauns and donkeys, may be surprised or disappointed that we haven't included any of that genre. Quite simply, such cod-Irishness is not in the ken of Dubliners or Irish people in general.

Dublin was predominantly an English city, with all the values that entails from the time it gained its royal charter in 1192 up to the early 19th century, when Catholic Emancipation marked the change in the power structures of the city. Fast-forward to the 20th century – Dublin went through a period of being an introverted, almost provincial and shabby place from the 1930s to the 1960s. Nowadays, despite the economic crisis (which, like all such, will surely end sometime), the city has grown to be a vibrant one. Everything –

shopping, architecture, cuisine, public transport and outlook – has changed. It is now a vibrant European capital. Some refer to the Irish as the 'Latins of the North' – they certainly have an empathy for and benefit from the links with Ireland's true mainland, the European continent. Our near neighbours need not worry either. As mentioned, Dublin was an English city for most of its time. Visit now to see its take on Georgian and (the much-neglected) Victorian architecture, ringing declarations of our British-influenced architectural heritage.

Dublin never had many smoke-stack industries in the last century. Now, it has become the European centre for the new economy: Facebook, Google, Microsoft and IBM have all placed their European headquarters there. While there is an underclass, perpetually unemployed, with squalor and drugs, the majority of the population include young well-educated people, working in high-tech, high-added-value industry.

Ireland has changed radically over the last ten years. Around 12 per cent of the population are foreigners (or 'non-nationals' as the term charmingly runs). According to the 2011 census Dublin's population is made up of 20 per cent non-nationals, a figure that rises to more than 70 per cent in the area around O'Connell Street at the centre of the city. Such is Dublin's skill at assimilating people from other nations, surely these newcomers, when they have settled down and become true 'Dubs', will generate a host of strange tales to add to the collection we have written about here (and we feel we have barely scratched the surface).

This book was written from on high, in Paddy's case from his splendid perch with a panoramic and perfect view down one of Dublin's well-preserved Victorian streets; one of Michael's perches is ensconced in Dublin Victoriana, while another was occasionally in Spain, looking out at Gibraltar (where Joyce's Edwardian protagonist, Molly Bloom, blossomed from girlhood in *Ulysses*).

Every writer needs a good editor, with a delicate touch on the tiller when necessary. Our literary lion was Malcolm Croft of Portico Books, and we are grateful to him for his assistance.

Finally, when you've read the book, why not come and experience the movie? Visit Dublin! To entice you, we quote from Michael's recent book, *50 Things to Do in Dublin*:

Introduction

Dublin is not a city running like a Swiss clock (sorry, Switzerland). Sometimes it's a bit chaotic. However, what raises the city above the ordinary are the people: they will engage with you. This is a social city. They are a friendly bunch, the Dubliners. They will talk to you. In a pub, shop, or on a bus they will have a conversation. In this vibrant, lively city, they will be (generally) helpful, sharp and witty.

There is a huge variety of things to see all around the city. Dublin has depth and soul, and, in the Spanish sense of magical quality, *duende*.

WELCOME TO BLACK POOL
AD 837

In ancient times, the sea and rivers were the super-highways and the best way to get from place to place. To travel overland was to venture through dark and misty forests with who knows what dangerous spirits lurking within. Those Norsemen from Scandinavia who took to raiding and trading became lords of the waters. Their initial voyages were to Iceland, Britain and Ireland. They excelled in warfare, with their spears, axes and swords. The dragon-prowed longships, constructed of strong oak planks, were able to endure the rigours of the North Atlantic. A shallow draught meant the Vikings could penetrate deep into the heart of a country, up rivers and into lakes.

Viking longships from Norway pulled into Dublin in AD 837. With its fine bay and strategic location, it offered a convenient base. The Vikings set up a trading fort near where the River Poddle flows into the Liffey, called Dubh Linn (black pool) – hence the name Dublin in English. In time Dublin became the most important Viking trading centre in the West. They raided many areas throughout Ireland, sailing up rivers and sacking what were then rich monasteries. Booty included gold, butter and corn. Monks prayed for bad weather and storms, all the better to give respite from the ferocious raiding parties.

Having brought the art of maritime raiding to an ever higher level, the Vikings ventured onwards to harry the coast of France. In 844, they sailed further south and attacked the Islamic state of Al-Andalus, which then extended over most of the Iberian Peninsula. Here was a land of plenty, ruled from Cordoba, then one of the most important cities in Europe. Lisbon was raided and they proceeded southwards around the Atlantic coast to the mouth of the River Guadalquivir. They sailed upriver and assaulted the great city of Seville. This was sacked and they gathered large amounts of booty.

They continued inland, but were met by the Amir and his army, who soundly routed the Vikings. The few surviving Vikings were rounded up; these sensibly converted to Islam. They settled down and became dairy farmers, producing a cheese that was in great demand in Seville and Cordoba.

In Ireland, coins from Al-Andalus have been found in excavations of a Viking settlement in the Waterford region. It is not known if these came from booty or trade. After the raids on the Iberian coast and peninsula, in Al-Andalus there was puzzlement about these strange people: who were they and what was their motivation? A delegation was sent by the Amir to Dublin, then the leading Viking strategic centre. Leaving the warm climes of the south, the emissaries would have encountered a greener but colder environment as they sailed into Dublin's great bay. They would have docked on the south of the river, entered the protective stockade and walked along the bustling passageways of the Viking settlement. Here were shops and craftsmen including busy weavers, bronze-workers and carpenters. The visitors were brought to meet Turgeis, the Norse king. It is regrettable that there is no record of the outcome of this remarkable meeting with the battle-hardened Norse chieftain. It must have been truly a clash of civilisations. One wonders what these representatives from sophisticated Cordoba, with its libraries of knowledge, great science, the exquisite Grand Mosque, public baths, running water and street lighting would have made of the settlement of Dublin and its powerful Norse ruler, ensconced in his post-and-wattle buildings along the muddy banks of the Liffey.

THE SECRET RIVER PODDLE
1000

Celtic eels, a penknife-wielding old woman who lived in the woods, one and a half Vikings and a helipad. James Joyce may have celebrated Anna Livia Plurabelle – the River Liffey – in *Finnegans Wake*, but Dublin has other rivers, some of them now hidden, and the mother of them all is the Poddle. To call it a river is a slight exaggeration: the name is probably ironic, and it is not by accident that if you change the first vowel you get 'piddle' or 'puddle'.

The Poddle was one reason for Dublin's existence, being where the Vikings used to beach their longships. The gently sloping bed of the mouth – or delta as it was – of the River Liffey allows the tide to flow up it for the best part of two miles, making it impossible to drink its salty water. For drinking water, the Vikings relied on the tiny Poddle. Though small, it was sufficient for their needs. At low tide the Poddle's outflow through a grating into the Liffey can be spied at Wellington Quay upriver from the Ha'penny Bridge. The city's other Gaelic name, Baile Átha Cliath, the 'city of the hurdle ford', was called after a ford across the Liffey near the mouth of the Poddle, using hurdles made of wattle and placed on piles of stones.

The Poddle was also used for defence: it formed part of the moat surrounding Dublin Castle, the centre of power for the Normans in the Pale – that part of the east of Ireland that they controlled – and later of English power in the whole of Ireland. The Poddle passes right through the Dublin Castle enclosure: it flows in by the Ship Street gate (so called because it was where sheep, not ships, were sold), along by the former moat, outside the two remaining southern towers, and through what was the Black Pool. This has now been converted into the Dubh Linn Garden, which features the shapes of eels mentioned in the early Irish sources as being found here. You can get a good look at the garden from the second floor of the

Chester Beatty Library. On closer inspection you will see that a number of red lights are spaced around the eels, and on the adjoining buildings, a reminder of unhappy times when for security reasons Margaret Thatcher, Prime Minister of the United Kingdom, had to be helicoptered in here to an EU summit meeting. It was almost 200 years before that the flag of the United Kingdom had been flown for the first time ever in the adjoining Upper Yard of Dublin Castle. When excavations were carried out here for the large new building at the corner of South Great George's Street and Longford Street, the remains of one Viking and half of another were found.

When more wells were opened around the expanding city, the Poddle suffered the indignity of being used as a sewer: hence its name in Irish, the Sáile (related to the word salach, dirty). It was in this guise that it is best known to Irish children, in the gory nursery song with the chorus Wee-le, Wee-le, Waw-le: There was an old woman, and she lived in the woods. She had a baby, three months old, which she finally kills by sticking a 'penknife in the baby's heart, down by the River Sáile'.

In the summer of 2012 several men were discovered in the middle of the night trying to descend into a manhole in Ship Street just outside Dublin Castle. It would have been very embarrassing if they had succeeded in getting inside the castle via the underground River Poddle: the castle is the home of the Special Branch of the Garda, the Irish Police!

CHRIST CHURCH AND
ITS ODD ARTEFACTS
1030

Christ Church Cathedral is located in the oldest part of Dublin. Splendidly situated, it sits on a commanding hill that overlooks the Liffey (save for a few bunker-like buildings in between that house the City Council headquarters, built in the concrete brutalist style of the late 1970s).

Brutalism of another kind may have been on the mind of Sitric Silkenbeard, Viking King of Dublin, in his daily affairs. However, more sublime matters may have motivated him when, after a pilgrimage to Rome, he arranged around 1030 for the construction of what turned into Christ Church. Most of the cathedral's oldest extant buildings were constructed by the Normans around 1200 and much building was carried out in the centuries that followed. In 1487, it was here that the boy pretender to the English throne, Lambert Simnel, was 'crowned' as Edward VI (see page 24). The victorious William of Orange paid a visit here after his victory at the Battle of the Boyne in July 1690. He thanked God and donated gilt plate, now on display in the Treasures of Christ Church exhibition in the 12th-century crypt.

By the 19th century the cathedral was in a ruinous state. Step forward the 'demon drink' (in the form of Henry Roe, a Dublin whiskey distiller) to the rescue. Mr Roe paid for a complete restoration of the cathedral and, with its mix of Victorian and medieval architecture, it is now an impressive place to visit. It formed a splendid backdrop when much of the television series, *The Tudors*, was filmed there, and some of the costumes used in the series are on display in the crypt.

Over the centuries the cathedral has gathered many artefacts, such as William of Orange's gilt plate and what is called Strongbow's tomb (see page 20). There are other items of a particularly strange nature. On display in a glass case are the mummified remains of an ancient cat and rat, preserved for eternity, in the middle of a chase. They were discovered in an organ during maintenance in the mid-19th century, where the dry air of the cathedral had preserved them. James Joyce, in his novel *Finnegans Wake*, referred to a person 'as stuck as that cat to that mouse in that tube of that Christchurch organ ...'

As one might expect, there are several plaques to Irishmen who have died in places across the Empire, for instance India in the British Army during the 19th century. However, much more curious is a rectangular urn, decorated with the bust of a man, that is discreetly set on a ledge in the southern aisle. A plaque below explains that here are the ashes of Major Marko Zekov Popovich, who died in London in 1934. It states that the good Major was the 'hereditary standard bearer of Montenegro'. It turns out that he was a well-known soldier and politician in the Balkans in the early part of the 20th century and had written books on the future of Montenegro. But what has Dublin got to do with Montenegro? Very little, is the answer. One suggestion is that a Montenegrin prince, who lived in the equally unlikely location of Limerick, arranged for Major Popovich's ashes to be placed in the cathedral.

Every church or cathedral needs a good relic or two. So what could be more appropriate than to have within Christ Church the preserved heart of Saint Lawrence O'Toole, who had been Archbishop of Dublin during the era of Strongbow in the 12th century? To cap it all, he was the first native Dubliner to hold the position, and is Dublin's patron saint. The sacred organ was placed in a heart-shaped wooden box, set behind iron bars at the rear of the cathedral. However, in a weird episode, the heart was stolen one night in March 2012. It seems the culprit secretly hid in the cathedral before closing time. The next morning, when the vergers opened the church, they noticed the theft of the relic – but they also noticed that two candles on the Trinity Altar had been lit during the night.

Despite the presence of much gold and silver, the thief had focused only on the relic, using strong shears to prise open the iron cage. Thus, in these materialist times, church officials speculated that the most likely motive was that it was carried out by that rare species, a religious fanatic.

THE NORMAN WISDOM OF STRONGBOW AND HIS SURPRISING DESCENDANT

1169

The name Strongbow means much more than a brand of cider. In real life the Norman leader Strongbow cast a long shadow over Dublin. He was in charge when the place developed from being a collection of wattle-hutted dwellings into the beginnings of a true city with substantial stone buildings, some of which are with us today. However, as we shall see, along the way Strongbow gained wealth and lands, as well as the fringe benefit of a princess for a wife. Prepare yourself for a shock when you see the speculation about a possible descendant.

We must first trace the long journey of the Normans from Normandy to Dublin. Like their forefathers, the Norsemen, the Normans were intrepid world travellers. In the 880s Vikings had parked their longships on the Normandy beaches and settled down in the green fields of northern France. After the usual intermarriage with the local Frankish wenches, it was time to think of far horizons, as there were kingdoms to conquer. These restless people cast their eyes on an island just over the horizon. It might be wet and damp, but booty, lands and estates called. So it was that the Anglo-Saxon King Harold and his army were overrun by the Norman steamroller at Hastings in 1066. The way was clear to set up their domain in England and Wales and assign lands to the various lords.

A hundred years later, the Irish King of Leinster, Diarmuid MacMurragh, had a problem and was in need of help. Love (albeit a rather rough version of it) was the basis of his troubles. Diarmuid had been ejected from his kingdom by the High King of Ireland in 1167, because he had abducted Devorgilla, the wife of a fellow king.

19

Diarmuid travelled through the Norman domains and met King Henry II in Aquitaine. Could someone come and help him – he would make it worthwhile? Henry was not madly enthused; the neighbouring island to the West looked rather dubious. Zut alors! It was even wetter than England! However, he did give a letter of support to Diarmuid, which allowed him to canvass support across western England and Wales.

After an unpromising start, he met Richard de Clare, 2nd Earl of Pembroke, also known as Strongbow. De Clare was receptive, having been deposed by the King from his lands in Pembroke, because he had sided against him in an earlier dispute. The trump card came when Diarmuid threw in the lure: an offer of marriage to his eldest daughter Aoife, with the promise of accession to the kingship of Leinster. Strongbow was hooked and he rounded up the usual knights and foot soldiers for the invasion of Ireland. The Norman army set out by ship and in 1169 quickly took the coastal towns of Wexford and Waterford. In the following year, Dublin was taken. Ironically, these had all been Viking settlements and the inhabitants would have been distant racial cousins of the Normans. Strongbow married Aoife after the landings and established himself in Dublin as Lord of Leinster. He died in 1176 and his tomb was placed in Christ Church Cathedral. However, when the roof collapsed in 1562, the tomb was damaged and the one that stands there today is a replica.

Diarmuid is still, to this day, regarded as the quintessential traitor in Ireland – having invited in an invader who ruled for 800 years.

Strongbow was probably the most successful warlord of his day. Nevertheless it came as something of a shock when local historians in Wexford claimed in 2005 to have discovered that one George W. Bush was descended from Strongbow (and thus of course from Aoife, daughter of the traitorous Diarmuid, King of Leinster). Bush has been called many names, warlord among them. Genes are a tricky thing, but if the genealogical research is true, the inclination to assemble a large army, invade a country and capture it was also successfully handed down.

FAIR DONNYBROOK: DONNYBROOK FAIR, DUBLIN 4

1204

The name Donnybrook has a very venerable history: in Irish Gaelic Domhnach Broc means the church of St Broc. The Old Irish name Domhnach is derived from the Latin Dominicus, 'of the Lord', and is one of the earliest names used for churches in Ireland.

To most Irish people nowadays Donnybrook signifies the headquarters of RTÉ (Raidió Teilifís Éireann, Ireland's national public service broadcaster), which moved to a site adjoining a house called Montrose, soon after its creation in 1960 and the start in 1962 of Irish television broadcasting. The radio service, which RTÉ also took over, moved from the General Post Office to a new building on the site in Donnybrook in 1973. Because of the huge technical changes involving digital technology, it is already in need of replacement.

To Leinster rugby fans, Donnybrook implies the stadium where the Old Wesley and Bective Rangers Rugby Union teams play. To the parents of Dublin teenagers, Donnybrook conjures up visions of minimally dressed daughters being collected from the Old Wesley disco on freezing winter nights. To Irish residents, 'Dublin 4', including Donnybrook, evokes the movers and shakers in Irish society, particularly those near the diplomatic quarter of Ailesbury and Shrewsbury Roads, in RTÉ, and in nearby UCD (University College Dublin, the largest university in Ireland, which moved from Earlsfort Terrace in the city centre to nearby Belfield over a number of decades from 1968 until very recently).

But outside Ireland, and especially in North America, a donnybrook refers to a riotous brawl, and recalls the famous

Donnybrook Fair. The term 'donnybrook' is hardly known in Ireland nowadays, however.

The fair had a long history: it was founded in 1204 by royal charter of King John of England. It was a major fixture in Dublin life for centuries, and was held initially for one week, soon extended to a fortnight, in August and September. The fairground straddled the River Dodder, at either side of which were large grounds devoted to the buying and selling of livestock, especially horses. The 1907 International Exhibition Grounds at Herbert Park, now a public park, also used some of the former fairgrounds.

But the real action was among the human alpha males: Donnybrook Fair became a site less for athletic competitions in the tradition of the ancient Tailteann Games (which long preceded even the ancient Greek Olympic Games), and more for interpersonal relations involving feats of drinking, boxing, wrestling, shillelagh-wielding and especially head-cracking. The shillelagh in those times was not a tourist trinket or souvenir. It consisted of a piece of blackthorn stick in two parts, joined in the middle by a leash. The Irish word is *saill éalaigh*: saill is a stick of blackthorn, *éalach* is a leash. The stick was sometimes weighted with lead, and if you received a blow from one on your noggin, it was time to consult the undertaker.

After Catholic Emancipation was granted in 1829 there was a great impulse to Catholicise Dublin and Ireland. It was felt by the city fathers, who could now include Catholics for the first time, and by the Archbishop of Dublin, Dr Cullen, that the annual happenings in Donnybrook would have to come to a rapid end. The problem was that the owner of the fair had a licence given by no less than a king, admittedly a dead one. In law, the licence would have to be bought out. A collection was made among the great and the good of Catholic Dublin to purchase the licence from its holder, a widow, for whom it was her only source of income.

And so it came to pass that the licence to hold the fair was bought up. The burghers of Dublin had another whip-round to build a church on the site of the former fair. The church – opened in 1866 – is a very large one, named in honour of the Sacred Heart of Jesus, and built in expiation of the many sins committed on the site over the previous centuries.

The horsey connections of Dublin Donnybrook did not peter out completely, however. In 1868, the Royal Dublin Society began to organise a huge horse show at the beginning of August . It soon became the major social event of the year, the highlight of the social season, when all the nobility in Ireland and their hangers-on came to Dublin to be presented at the court in Dublin Castle. In 1922, after independence, the RDS sold its property at Leinster House, which faced onto both Kildare Street and Merrion Square. The new state converted it into the new houses of the Oireachtas, the Irish legislature. The RDS moved out to Ballsbridge, next to Donnybrook, and it is here that it holds its annual horse show, the biggest international event of its type in Ireland.

On the other sides of the Dodder, also on the former fairground, the then newly arrived game of Rugby Union rapidly became the pitches for the Old Wesley and Bective Rangers teams.

The construction of the Donnybrook bus garage in 1951, a building with the largest use of concrete shell roofing in Ireland, ensured that the revellers of Donnybrook Fair will never be able to return.

IN THE FIRST YEAR OF OUR REIGN: RAISING THE YORKIST BAR IN DUBLIN
1487

The Wars of the Roses was a complicated series of dynastic civil wars in England between the houses of York and Lancaster. The root of all this was that both houses claimed the throne through their lineage from King Edward III. Dublin was fated to provide a stage for one of the last parts of the conflict. The event started when one Lambert Simnel, the son of a joiner, was chosen by an Oxford priest for his resemblance to one of the Yorkist 'princes in the tower', who were last seen alive in 1483. The priest trained the youth in courtly ways, but then changed his mind about the imposter's identity and put forward the idea that he was Edward, Earl of Warwick, a cousin to the princes in the tower with claims of his own to the throne. The real Warwick was a prisoner of the present king Henry VII, established in power after his victory at Bosworth Field. The rumour of Warwick's escape spread and Henry VII was forced to take his real prisoner from the tower and parade him through London. Irrespective of this, the conspiracy gained momentum. The Oxford priest transported the hapless 12-year-old Simnel to Ireland, a sympathetic location, as most of the Irish Anglo-Norman nobility supported the Yorkist side.

On 24 May 1487, a grand ceremony was held, which in reality was the surreal elevation of an imposter to kinghood. Simnel was brought to Christ Church Cathedral, built on a hill overlooking the Liffey in Dublin, the principal cathedral of the Irish kingdom. Here, in this magnificent building, the young boy was crowned King Edward VI of England, Ireland and France. It is said that he was crowned with a tiara removed from a statue of the Virgin Mary in a Dublin church. He was acclaimed by the Irish nobility and Gerald, Earl of Kildare, as

Lord Deputy of Ireland, presided at the ceremony. Later, the freshly crowned King got down to royal business. He signed various decrees that were put in front of him, appointing various personages under the new disposition. They were in the style of 'Edward, by the grace of God, King of England, France and Ireland, to all to whom these presents may come, greeting' and ended with the kingly 'in the first year of our reign'.

A king's life is a busy one so he had to set off immediately to England to deal with some unfinished business. A large force, comprising English and Irish Yorkists as well as Flemish mercenaries sent by the Holy Roman Emperor, was quickly assembled. With the pretender in tow, this force sailed for England on 4 June and landed in Lancashire. The opposing armies met at Stoke on 16 June, where the Yorkists were soundly defeated and Simnel was captured. Henry VII recognised that the youth was only a harmless pawn in the conspiracy and spared him. Simnel spent the rest of his days as a turnspit in the royal kitchens, a long way from his brief but halcyon time when, clad in royal ermine, he was transported through the Dublin streets to great acclaim.

DUPLICITOUS DETENTION AND DEATH IN A FROZEN VALLEY

1591

Enter the historic surroundings of Dublin Castle and head to the Lower Yard. In the background, adjacent to the Chapel Royal, you see the high and slightly sinister lines of the Record Tower. You can easily guess what it once was: a place of imprisonment. Originally built in the 13th century, it is tall and cylindrical with 12ft-thick grey limestone walls, topped by a battlemented parapet. The tower now houses the rather cluttered museum of the Garda Síochána, the Irish police force – the museum is worth a visit. As a bonus you can experience there the wonderful spiral staircase that transports you to the atmospheric rooms set at different levels.

Dublin Castle had been at the centre of control of Ireland since it was built by the Anglo-Normans. Thus the unfortunates who were incarcerated in the Record Tower would usually have been important rebels. This was the case when Red Hugh O'Donnell was locked up here during the 16th century. The background to this was Queen Elizabeth's resolve to subdue the Kingdom of Ireland and stamp out rebellion. The population there adhered to Catholicism and English rule only applied to parts of the country. There was the underlying fear that Ireland would be used as a base by Spain to attack England.

Elizabeth's Lord Deputy in Ireland, Sir John Perrot, was not her favourite person. After an unsuccessful foray against rebels she chillingly wrote: 'Let us have no more such rash, unadvised journeys without good ground as your last journey in the north ... Take heed ere you use so again.' So what was Sir John to do? In a scenario as outlandish as something out of *Blackadder* he hit upon a scheme that would give him leverage in the struggle to subdue the rebellious northern lords. He decided to kidnap Red Hugh, son of Hugh O'Donnell, a Gaelic lord and member of one of the pre-eminent Irish aristocratic families in the North of the country. In 1587, he dispatched a ship from Dublin. It made its way north and sailed into Lough Swilly. There, the captain let it be known that the ship had wine for trade. The young Red Hugh and his companions were invited on board to sample the wine. In the middle of feasting, the grim reality dawned: the hatches were closed and the young lord was transported in chains to Dublin and thence to the Record Tower.

Red Hugh made an attempt to escape in 1591. He got as far as the foothills of the mountains, where the resident clan, the O'Tooles, fearful of retribution from the English, brought him back to Dublin Castle. Red Hugh's second attempt, accompanied by the brothers Art and Henry O'Neill, was successful. In the depths of winter in January 1592 the trio were smuggled by a guard through a privy and out of the castle. They made their way south, heading for the safety of the remote valley of Glenmalure, deep in the Wicklow Mountains, where the chieftain Fiach MacHugh O'Byrne held sway. The fugitives made their way through deep boggy valleys and over bleak mountains. They had no cloaks and only light clothing. As they progressed with difficulty, Art O'Neill (described as being a trifle corpulent) was not able to cope with sub-zero temperatures and the falling snow. At the base of a high cliff, he succumbed to hypothermia and passed into a coma. A message was sent to O'Byrne to get help. When O'Byrne's men found the fugitives they were only discernible as mounds covered in snow. Art died in the valley and was buried there. Red Hugh, a young fit man, was in better shape and carried to O'Byrne's stronghold on a litter. Nevertheless, he lost both big toes to frostbite. This escape was the only successful one from Dublin Castle in all its history.

As it happened, the scheming Sir John Perrot came to a bad end – he spent his last days in the Tower of London. Red Hugh went on to command rebel armies against the encroaching English rule. In 1601, the Spanish landed forces at Kinsale and Red Hugh marched his army to Munster to join their forces. The Kinsale invasion was defeated and Red Hugh subsequently went into exile in Spain, where he died in 1602.

Only an experienced hill walker could venture into the heart of the Wicklow Mountains to see the last vestiges of that desperate flight on a frozen winter night. Walking along the Kings River in the midst of conifer forests you turn into the isolated Glenreemore Valley. On the southern side there is a simple stone plaque set in the base of the cliff, where the inscription commemorates the death of Art O'Neill. Hundreds of feet above, near the edge of an escarpment, there is a large cross crafted in timber, visible from all around, known as Art's Cross. It marks the remote and lonely place where a 16th-century fugitive from Dublin Castle met his poignant end, only a few mountain ridges away from welcoming sanctuary.

ANATOMISED:
THE TEMPLE BAR ELEPHANT
1681

While many of today's late-night visitors to Dublin's right-bank Temple Bar area appear to be 'elephants'[1] one of the strangest facts about this recently rediscovered tourist area is that a very large African elephant was the subject of an elaborate anatomy lesson there, right in the middle of Essex Street, in 1681.

This animal was not one of Hannibal's African elephants that had strayed from his trip over the Alps in 220 BC. Its owner, a Mr Wilkins, had brought it to Ireland (since we have no native elephants, snakes, or moles here – not since the time of St Patrick!) for exhibiting, in an effort to make some quick money. Unfortunately, and inexplicably, soon after its arrival, the specially constructed wooden booth in which the huge animal was kept caught fire, along with its contents, and the unfamiliar smell of burning elephant emanated from its abode near the old Custom House on the corner of Parliament Street and Essex Street.

This posed a major problem for the owner: his investment had for all practical purposes gone up in smoke, and all he had to show for it was a large quantity of roasted elephant flesh. Undaunted, he came up with a cunning plan: rather than making a mountain out of a molehill, he resolved on making a packet out of a burned elephant corpse.

He decided his best option would be to put the elephant's skeleton on display: thus he couldn't afford to lose any of its corpse. He quickly sent for a troop of musketeers, who were ordered to guard the dead animal by force of arms. With quick thinking, he managed

[1] Rhyming slang: 'elephant's trunk' = drunk.

to cover up the scene of the pyre from the prying eyes and grasping hands of souvenir hunters, and he posted advertisements around the city, to the effect that the world's first anatomical dissection of an elephant would take place in Essex Street on 17 June.

Wilkins was fortunate in that there were many butchers living in the vicinity, and he enrolled these to take all the flesh from the elephant's corpse. They were sharpening their long meat-knives when a Dr Allan Mullen arrived at 8 p.m. Mullen was a graduate of Trinity College Dublin and would go on to be elected a member of the highly prestigious Royal Society in London, and was very keen on everything to do with anatomy. The idea of missing the opportunity of carrying out a proper dissection on this creature was anathema to him. He would have preferred to have gathered a team of anatomists to do the job properly, but the elephant – like Lazarus in his tomb – was beginning to go distinctly 'off'. Its proximity to some of the city's important buildings was likely to trigger swift action by the authorities.

Finally, Wilkins decided to allow Dr Mullen to supervise the work, provided it was done without further delay. So it was that after a long June evening Dublin's very first elephant dissection began by candlelight. The local butchers, despite the speed of their knifework, took a long time to get through the vast mountain of flesh and muscle that had ended up so curiously in the middle of the city. Mullen was meticulous in noting all the details of the operation and managed to have his observations published the following year on 12 May, entitled: 'An anatomical account of the elephant accidentally burnt in Dublin on Fryday, June 17 in the year 1681 sent in a letter to Sir William Petty, fellow of the Royal Society: together with a relation of new anatomical observations in the eyes of animals, communicated in another letter to the Honourable R. Boyle ... fellow of the same society / by A.M.'

What happened to the elephant's skeleton, however, remains a mystery. I wonder, dear reader, as you consume your Irish stew, where it could have ended up?

MUMMIES AND MORTALITY
1685

St Michan's Church, just north of the Liffey on Church Street, dates from 1095. As most of the development of Dublin in its early years was to the south of the river, St Michan's was the only parish church on the north side of the city over a period of six centuries. It was rebuilt in 1685 during the great expansion of Dublin that commenced when the Duke of Ormonde was Viceroy. Parishes in those times took their duties of safeguarding the morals of their flock very seriously. In the early 18th century the grounds of St Michan's held a pair of stocks, in which miscreants could be put for punishment. It is not recorded if they were used when the aptly named Thomas Vice was appointed by the vestry to investigate the ill-behaviour of men of the parish who were found to frequent brothels.

George Frideric Handel practised on the organ here (presumably *his* morals were found to pass muster!). This was before his 'Messiah' premiere, which was held on 13 April 1742 in Neal's Musick Hall in Fishamble Street, to the south of the river. The original organ case (dating from 1725, by J. Baptiste de Couville) as used by Handel is still there.

If you visit St Michan's, prepare yourself for some curious emotions. This is where you can reflect on your mortality and get a feel of where we humans are all heading! Take the tour to see the several burial vaults that are to be found below the church. Here, in the vaults, centuries-old bodies can be seen in a remarkable state of preservation. In one of the vaults you see, in open coffins, four mummified bodies. One of these is reputedly a Crusader who had to be sawn in half to fit into the coffin. The conservation of bodies is attributed to the tannic emanations from a nearby ancient buried oak forest, combined with the limestone walls and dry atmosphere.

For more of the macabre, enter another vault. Here you see the coffins of the Sheares brothers. These brothers were barristers who took part in the 1798 rising against British rule. Captured, they were tried and sentenced to death by the Crown for their part in the rising. The gruesome requirements for the manner in which they were to be executed, namely to be hanged, but not to death, then drawn and quartered, are spelled out in detail in the death sentence document, which is on display in the vault.

Thus, beneath the quiet environs of this church, the vaults are replete with mummies, mortality and visions of horror. It is not surprising that Dubliner Bram Stoker (1847–1912) is said to have come here to this peculiar place and was inspired to write his Gothic novel, *Dracula*.

BARBARY PIRATES, MERCHANT PRINCES AND 'OUZELERS'

1695

In 1983 a stamp was issued by the Irish Post Office depicting the 'Ouzel Galley Goblet'. The occasion was to commemorate the bicentenary of the Dublin Chamber of Commerce. So far, so commercial. It is good that this fine body of merchant princes are commemorated, but what is 'Ouzel' or the relevance of this fine glass goblet? There is more: James Joyce mentions it in *Finnegans Wake*: '... or carried of cloud from land of locust, in ouzel galley borne'.

The story of the ship, the *Ouzel Galley*, has similarities with the *Marie Celeste*, although it predates it by almost two centuries. It harks back to a time when commerce was hazardous and piracy rife. We begin with the known facts. In 1695, the *Ouzel Galley* sailed out of Ringsend at the entrance of Dublin harbour on a voyage to the port of Smyrna (now Izmir in Turkey), one of the foremost trading centres of the Ottoman Empire. The unusual name 'ouzel' means blackbird (from Middle English osle). The ship had been dispatched by the Dublin merchant house of Ferris, Twigg and Cash. There was an experienced crew of 37 and the captain, Eoghan Massey, came from Waterford. Normally a ship would have been expected to return from such a voyage in around a year but as the years dragged on there was no sign of it. By 1698 the reasonable assumption was made that the ship had been lost at sea or taken into captivity. The insurance underwriters duly paid compensation to the owners.

In 1700, five years after she had departed, the *Ouzel Galley* sailed back into Dublin Bay, her holds replete with spices and other treasure. The crew told of an amazing experience. They had been captured by Algerian corsairs and brought in captivity to the Barbary (North African) Coast. The ship and crew had been pressed into piracy, harrying shipping in the Mediterranean. One night, they recounted, the corsairs got drunk in their pirate lair. The Irish crew duly seized the moment, overwhelmed their captors and made their escape.

There were several consequences of this astonishing adventure. Many of the crew found that their wives, thinking their husbands were dead, had remarried and had children from their new marriage. It is said that to this day in Ringsend (now a suburb of Dublin), children born out of wedlock are known as 'ouzelers'. In the business world, there was a problem too: the insurance money had been paid out, so who should receive payment for the ship and its cargo? Litigation commenced and eventually it was decided to set up an arbitration process rather than see the money in question disappear into the deep pockets of the legal profession. In 1705, the matter was submitted to a specially formed group of merchants for adjudication and was settled. The Ouzel Galley Society was then established as a permanent arbitration body in Dublin, limited to a total of 40 members. Unusually for a body of august merchant princes, the officers of the society were designated as a ship's crew with officers and hands. This 'crew' comprised the captain, lieutenants, master, boatswain and carpenter etc. It would appear that as well as fulfilling the necessary arbitration duties, they were in line with the sea-going traditions of great dinners and copious drink, hence the Ouzel Galley Goblet! Eventually the need for such a unique mercantile club died away and the Dublin Chamber of Commerce was subsequently established.

Back to the voyage of the *Ouzel Galley*. It did not take long for the crew's extraordinary story to be examined in some detail. Undoubtedly, activities of Barbary pirates were at their peak during the 17th century. (Had not the unfortunate inhabitants of the village of Baltimore in West Cork been carried off into slavery by pirates from Algiers in 1631?) There were ports like Salé (near Rabat in present-day Morocco) that had brought the art of piracy to an unparalleled degree of sophistication (purpose-built shipyards producing fast agile galleys, advanced navigational equipment fitted, warehouses groaning with booty) – hence in England pirates were referred to as 'Sally Rovers'.

But, hang on a minute, said the Dublin sceptics. They declared the tale of the five-year captivity was fanciful. However, the alternative scenario proposed was even more incredible. Allegations were made that, in reality, the crew and ship had spent the intervening period in the West Indies, themselves acting as pirates. As it happens, the late 17th century, with a resurgence in Spanish output from the mines of Latin America and the rise of the sugar industry, is regarded as being the 'Golden Age of Piracy' in the Caribbean. Nevertheless, the matter was never resolved and the exact circumstances of the voyage of the *Ouzel Galley* remain shrouded in mystery.

A novel entitled *The Missing Ship, The Log of the Ouzel Galley* by one W.H.G. Kingston was published in the latter half of the 19th century. This was a stirring tale of derring-do, with heroes, the *Ouzel Galley* sailing through the West Indies, slaves saying 'Massa', and the French and the Spanish being seen off. Whatever the truth, a permanent vestige of this strange tale is still to be seen in central Dublin, where there is a fine stone plaque depicting the ship over the entrance to the former Commercial Buildings (once a meeting place of the Dublin Chamber of Commerce) at College Green.

VELLUM, CAGES AND CAPES
1701

Most books nowadays are quite reasonably priced. Nevertheless, libraries and bookshops have devised all sorts of elaborate security systems to prevent theft of their stock. Usually these are based on electronics and include magnetic cards, CCTV or both.

Now cast your mind back 300 years. Books then were expensive, rare, difficult to print and only available in rarefied circles like scholars' libraries. Books are very portable, easy to hide under one's cloak. Thus, what was a prudent librarian to do when setting up a large library? This was the question that energised Dr Narcissus Marsh, when he was establishing the library (now known as Marsh's Library) that nestles at the side of St Patrick's Cathedral in Dublin. (And if you think Narcissus was a peculiar name, how about those of his brothers: Epaphroditus and Onesiphorus?)

Marsh was Archbishop of Dublin and in 1701, dissatisfied with the arrangements for scholars in Trinity College, he paid for the establishment of the library using his own funds. When it was founded, it was the first public library in Ireland. The library contains a priceless collection of 25,000 books on all the known subjects of the time. The first librarian, Dr Bouhéreau, was a Huguenot who had fled France in 1695. He left his collection to the library, part of which is now an important source for the study of Calvinism in 17th-century France. The collections are still shelved as they were allocated by Marsh and Bouhéreau. It is possible to visit the library (still a working one), which has been called a treasury of the European mind. Come here if you want to savour the experience of early 18th-century Dublin.

Marsh solved the question of protecting his priceless collection of books in two ways. Firstly, many of the books were chained. Each had a small metal clasp linked to a chain that ran on a wooden rod attached to each shelf. The next arrangement was more effective but definitely idiosyncratic – it smacked more of the gaoler than the librarian. In a gallery at the rear of the library three elegant wired alcoves or 'cages' were established. Thus, hundreds of years ago, you, gentleperson scholar, could breeze into the library, doff your hat, cape and sword. One of Dr Bouhéreau's assistants would lead you to the rear and lock you into your cage. You would select your books from the shelves within the cage; delve through the dusty and learned paper and vellum; read to your heart's content in the flickering candlelight; savour the knowledge encapsulated here, gathered from all across the known world. Afterwards, mind refreshed and full of knowledge, you depart, with no danger of larceny!

TALES OF THE HELLFIRE CLUB, BUCKS AND THE HOLY CITY
1725

The Hellfire Club is set on a hill in the Dublin Mountains. Partly wooded now, it is pleasant to take a weekend stroll here and admire the view of Ireland's capital, the great sprawling metropolis far below. However, on a winter's night during the 18th century this isolated structure would have presented a barren, bleak prospect. A rather sombre, squat, stone building, it has a roof also constructed of stone. It was built as a hunting lodge by William Conolly (speaker of the Irish Parliament) in 1725. Peter Somerville-Large, in his book *Dublin*, tells that later it became the Hellfire Club, which was disbanded in 1741 after its main protagonist, Lord Rosse, who was enamoured of all the 'vices which the beau monde calls pleasures', died. This club provided a location for the aristocratic and rich 'young bucks' to carouse in. What went on there is a topic of much speculation, whether it was merely drinking and gambling, or – as is often darkly hinted – occult rites. There is even a tale of a dark cat that haunts the hill – the Devil in feline form.

Down below the mountains, Dublin grew enormously in Georgian times. By the end of the 18th century it was the second city of the two kingdoms, after London. The fashionably dressed bucks caroused around the elegant squares and gracious terraces of the city. The many taverns and gambling houses were their habitual haunts. Bravado was all. One Dublin shop had walking sticks on offer for these young men inscribed with slogans like 'Who dare sneeze' or 'Who's afraid'. Duels were frequent and they even jostled passers-by to try and demand satisfaction and thus a duel.

Thomas 'Buck' Whaley was the best known of these 18th-century rakes. Born in 1766, he was the son of a wealthy landowner,

Richard Chapell Whaley. The father had gained notoriety for religious intolerance against Catholics. He was a priest-hunter known as 'Burn Chapel'. Not having adhered to his studies, young Thomas was sent to Paris in his teens to be sorted out. By the time he returned to Ireland, he had honed his skills as a libertine. He was elected as Member of Parliament to the Irish House of Commons in 1785. On his father's death he inherited a fortune and, now enormously rich, devoted his time to squandering his fortune by drinking and revelry. So far, so normal in the everyday life of a rake.

In an unexpected and curious move, Whaley decided to rise above the humdrum existence of living it up. In 1788 he made a wager that he could travel to Jerusalem and back within a year. To travel to the Holy City, at the other end of the Mediterranean, and ensconced within the Ottoman Empire, was an extraordinarily difficult journey, particularly within that time limit. So, the intrepid Whaley set out. Nothing was heard until he duly returned 10 months later, to be greeted by bonfires in celebration of his great feat. He pocketed a reported £15,000 in wagers, an enormous sum for the time. Whaley had more adventures, and continued dissipating his money, eventually spending time in a debtors' prison.

He died in 1800 in Cheshire, while travelling to London. He had written his memoirs (published posthumously) with the intent of dissuading young men from following his example and where he confessed to having 'ridiculous pretensions to notoriety'.

MADAM STEEVENS:
THE ORIGINAL 'MISS PIGGY'?
1733

In the late 1980s a high wall across the road from Heuston Station
(as Kingsbridge was officially renamed in 1966) was demolished,
and Dubliners were amazed when a beautifully restored building
emerged for all to see. For years it was known as 'Dr Steevens's
Hospital'. For much of its existence as a hospital, however, it was not
so much its architectural beauty or the skill of its doctors that kept
the local populace chatting about it. For the people of Dublin knew
there was a weird story attached to this building, and every one of
them could swear on the Bible that it was true!

Grizel (short for Grizelda) Steevens – along with her twin
brother, Richard – was born in England in 1653. The family had
fled from Cromwell's Puritans to Ireland while the twins were still
infants. In 1710 her brother died and she inherited a large income
for as long as she lived. After her own death the money was to be
used to found a hospital for 'sick and wounded persons whose
distempers and wounds are curable'. But Grizel determined to set it
up during her lifetime and spent much of her own money on the first
voluntary hospital in Dublin, which opened in 1733 and was called
Dr Steevens's Hospital after her brother.

Grizel Steevens, who was usually known as Madam Steevens,
suffered for lack of a good public relations officer. A rumour arose
that she had the head of a pig. Her mother, when pregnant with her,
had supposedly chased away a beggar with many children, and called
them little pigs. She was punished – so the story went – by giving
birth to her daughter Grizel, with a pig's head on her shoulders.

There was a fad around this time for stories about rich women
with pigs' heads. But while these women were figments of the

imagination, Grizel Steevens was a real person. In fact, she suffered from an eye condition and used to wear a veil to prevent it from getting worse. In an effort to scotch the rumours, she would sit on her balcony in the sun, for all to see. She even had her portrait painted to prove that she had a perfectly normal human face. This picture was hung in the entrance hall of the hospital, and is still on view. She died in 1746 but the porcine legend lived on after her.

Political correctness not yet having been invented, visitors to the hospital were even shown the silver trough from which – so it was said – Grizel Steevens used to eat. They were also shown a picture of her with a pig's head. When William Wilde, father of Oscar Wilde, began his training as a surgeon in Dr Steevens's Hospital in 1832, he was also shown the silver trough. The legend continued right down to the middle of the 20th century.

The Dr Steevens Hospital Act of 1729 had allowed for the setting up of the hospital. It was not until 1961 that the body corporate established by the Act and the board for Dr Steevens's Hospital were dissolved and ceased to exist. In the end, after nearly 230 years of fulfilling her wishes, Grizel Steevens surely had the last laugh.

THE BRIAN BORÚ HARP IN THE LONG ROOM IN TCD

1760

'If any of your readers want to see a perfect specimen of an Irish harp, let them go to Trinity College Museum.' Thus proclaimed the *Dublin Penny Journal* on New Year's Day, 1832.

Suppose you've just visited the Book of Kells; you've climbed the steps up to the Long Room, one of the most beautiful architectural spaces in Europe, you marvel at all the galleries of books reaching to the high roof in this gorgeous interior. Now make sure you don't miss the BrianBorú harp! Presented to the College in 1760 by William Conyngham, it's a rare and revered item: there are only three such harps in existence. BrianBorú (High King of Ireland 1002–14) was long dead, however, by the time it was made.

Rewinding a bit, every Irish schoolchild knows the (mythical) story of Labhraidh Loingseach, who suffered from a highly embarrassing bodily ailment: ass's ears. Of course, he had on occasions to get his very long hair cut, but in such a way that his secret remained hidden. He had to keep moving from barber to barber because, after paying and tipping them, he had each one killed. The widowed mother of one young barber, an only child, persuaded Labhraidh to spare her son. Keeping this terrible secret was too much for the young man, however, and he consulted the local druid, who advised him to tell his story to a tree, and so get cured. A few years afterwards, the tree was felled and turned into a harp, which ended up in the hands of Labhraidh's harper. While the harper was playing to the assembled clan, the harp began to sing and told everyone about Labhraidh's secret. Labhraidh was deeply ashamed for his barber-victims, repented, and thereafter let everyone know about his ear problem.

The Vikings loved the sound of the harp from the time of their arrival in Ireland, and it has always been associated with Irish national identity. After the Norman-Welsh invasion of 1169, Norman-Irishmen were forbidden to play the Irish harp or speak Gaelic.

In the 13th to 15th centuries, the golden age of the harp, harpers were aristocrats, employed at the courts of the Gaelic chieftains. The pecking order at this time was: chieftain, poet, harper. Under the (Gaelic) Brehon laws there were heavy fines for upsetting a harper. If you broke a harper's nail, the fine was four cows, a substantial sum (then as now).

The so-called Brian Ború harp is three feet high, and bears Celtic carvings and precious stones. It emits a beautifully melting and resonantly gorgeous sound. Catgut was not used; indeed, several replicas have been made of it with strings of metal: brass wire, silver or even gold. This kind of early Irish harp was in use up to the end of the 18th century. Irish song, often accompanied by the harp, was of one of three types: *suantraí*, the lullaby; *goltraí*, the sad song; and *geantraí*, the happy one. (At a later stage the Dubliner John Field invented yet another form of music, *nochtraí*, the nocturne.)

From the time of King Henry VIII, the harp was used as a symbol of Ireland, and still appears on the UK's insignia (in respect of Northern Ireland). During Ireland's darkest days, the unstrung harp was used as a symbol of the broken nation. The poet Thomas Moore (1779–1852, famous for his 'Moore's Melodies') also loved the harp. His beautiful poem, 'The Harp that Once through Tara's Halls', set to an old air, evokes this period with nostalgia:

> The harp that once through Tara's halls
> The soul of music shed,
> Now hangs as mute on Tara's walls
> As if that soul were fled.
> So sleeps the pride of former days,
> So glory's thrill is o'er,
> And hearts that once beat high for praise,
> Now feel that pulse no more!

No more to chiefs and ladies bright
The harp of Tara swells;
The chord alone that breaks at night,
Its tale of ruin tells.
Thus Freedom now so seldom wakes,
The only throb she gives
Is when some heart indignant breaks,
To show that still she lives.

After independence in 1922, this very harp, facing left, was adopted as the national emblem of Ireland. It appears on all State correspondence (even tax demands), on shields outside all Irish embassies and consulates, and on Irish currency (when Ireland had its own notes) and Irish euro-currency coins. On older notes, Lady Hazel Lavery, the wife of Irish painter Sir John Lavery, was depicted in Irish national costume – in the guise of Hibernia, the personification of Ireland – with her chin resting on her hand and leaning on an Irish harp. Ireland is the only country in the world to have a musical instrument as its emblem, reflecting the national passion for all types of music.

The Irish Free State, and from 1949 the Republic, was not however the first entity to use the harp as its emblem. Arthur Guinness, who established his brewing business in Dublin in 1759, got there first: the company registered it, in its right-facing form, as their trademark in 1862. A century later, they even introduced a lager called Harp.

The traditional music of Ireland had taken a back seat by the mid-20th century. However, in the 1960s, a Corkman, Seán Ó Riada, fascinated by the works of the blind harper and composer Turlough O'Carolan (1670–1738), tried to reproduce the sounds of the old metal-stringed harp by using the harpsichord. He founded the group Ceoltóirí Chualann, which later became The Chieftains, organised to play along the lines of a classical music ensemble. The rest was history: Derek Bell (1935–2002) took to playing the harp with the Chieftains, and the instrument was back to stay. Bell was a Belfastman; highly appropriate, as a major harpers' festival was held there in 1792.

Many of the smaller harps used in Ireland today are made in Japan, where they are often played by groups of harpists. In Irish usage, a harper is a traditional musician, whereas a harpist is a classical practitioner. Many harpers had suffered blindness, either from birth (often caused by alcohol destroying the optic nerve during pregnancy, or by German measles), or else from smallpox. Turlough O'Carolan was one such. Indeed Derek Bell had been misdiagnosed in childhood as suffering from an illness that would bring on blindness, and hence his parents sought to have him trained in playing the harp.

A replica of the Brian Ború harp was played in the Long Room by Siobhan Armstrong for Queen Elizabeth II during her very successful State visit to Ireland in May 2011. Like that of the President of Ireland, the Queen's car was decorated with a standard pennant bearing a heraldic Irish harp.

A LOT OF BULL AND THE ISLAND
BOUNTY OF CAPTAIN BLIGH
1768

Dublin has a wide and scenic bay. However, manoeuvring your ship here and securing safe moorings has been a problem over the centuries. The Liffey was shallow at its mouth, with extensive slob lands – very silty areas – at either side of the harbour entrance. Ringsend, a narrow spit of land on the south bank of the Liffey, developed as a fishing village from the 17th century onwards. Sailing ships docked here and, to get to the centre of Dublin, disembarking passengers had to take a Ringsend Car, a basic passenger carriage, traverse the low ground and make the difficult passage over the fickle River Dodder. The Pigeon House at Ringsend (named after John Pidgeon, who opened it), a fine granite hotel, was developed later in the 18th century to cater for the needs of weary passengers alighting from the packet boats that plied from Chester in England.

A primitive sea wall, made of oak piles, had been built during the early 18th century, in an eastwards direction. The intention of the wall was to provide protection for the harbour. The Poolbeg Lighthouse was built at the end of the wall in 1768. As the timber piles did not last due to wave action, a granite causeway was built towards the land. The granite was hewn from Dalkey Hill to the South, transported by boat and carefully placed, block by block, along the length of what became known as the Great South Wall (also known as the South Bull Wall), set in the hub of Dublin Bay. A walk along its length today, around a mile and a half over the undulating granite surface, offers great views, good exercise and copious bracing sea air. However, there remained problems with the port. The Liffey and harbour were still not easily navigable. As ships got bigger, there was not the draught for them to proceed further upriver.

For this difficult problem, there was need for an expert, one with experience of tides, the flow of water and surveying. The man who answered the call was one with remarkable experience. Step forward one Captain William Bligh. During the 'Mutiny on the Bounty' incident of 1789, he and his loyal followers had been set adrift in a 23-foot open boat in the Pacific by Fletcher Christian and his fellow mutineers. Bligh had no navigating instruments, only a quadrant and a pocket watch. By adroit navigation, over the space of 47 days and travelling over 4,000 miles, he managed to bring the boat to safety at Timor in the Dutch East Indies. Captain Bligh had thus earned a justifiable reputation for his navigation and surveying skills.

He was invited to survey Dublin Bay and came there in September 1800. After careful measurement and consideration he proposed a wall on the north side of the channel, parallel to the South Wall. This would speed the flow of water from the River Liffey, thus increasing natural scour, to deepen the shipping channel. His proposal was adopted and the North Bull Wall was completed in 1830 to his specifications. Construction of the two great sea walls had the desired effect and the channel was cleared. Ships could now sail closer to the commercial heart of the city. The resultant silt from the river flowed in a northwards direction, to form a new island, the Bull Island. Golfers, bathers and seabirds now enjoy its sandy shores, with no knowledge of the role the stern and dexterous Captain Bligh played in the island's creation.

DUBLIN'S 19TH-CENTURY STATUES: ROYALTY, POETS AND GELIGNITE
1809

Dublin's statues have always generated comment or, on occasion, a significantly more robust reaction. In James Joyce's great novel *Ulysses*, Leopold Bloom pauses by the statue of the Dublin poet and songwriter Thomas Moore, located in College Street above a public urinal, and muses: 'They did right to put him up over a urinal: meeting of the waters.' One of Moore's more famous songs is indeed about the 'Meeting of the Waters', which is where two rivers meet to form the River Avoca, in County Wicklow.

There are several statues in Dublin by John Henry Foley. Born in Dublin in 1818, Foley was a highly successful sculptor with commissions in Ireland, Britain and Imperial India. It could be said that he ran with the fox and hunted with the hounds. He was successful in securing commissions to produce statues of Irish nationalist figures like Daniel O'Connell (located in Dublin's O'Connell Street) as well as gaining the patronage of Queen Victoria, who visited him in his London studio in 1854. After the death of Prince Albert, the elaborate Albert Memorial was erected in London and Foley was commissioned to produce the gilt bronze statue of Albert in the centre of the monument. When Foley died in 1874, he was buried in the crypt of St Paul's Cathedral.

College Green is just around the corner from Moore's eyrie in College Street. Two statues by Foley are here: Edmund Burke (parliamentarian, writer on democracy and freedom) and Oliver Goldsmith (the poet and playwright: *She Stoops to Conquer, The Deserted Village*) in front of their alma mater, Trinity College; and, in a central position facing the old Irish Parliament, the figure of the great Irish parliamentarian Henry Grattan. An odd thing is that the muscular and well-defined legs on each of the figures are remarkably similar. This did not escape the attention of the Dublin wits at the time – they claimed that he had cast the legs from the same moulds.

Foley was commissioned to create another statue to Prince Albert in Dublin. After some controversy this elegant statue now sits partly obscured behind a hedge at the side of Leinster Lawn, in front of Leinster House, now home to Ireland's Parliament. A large statue of Queen Victoria was positioned in 1908 on the other side of Leinster House. In 1948, as Ireland was, in effect, under new management, the statue (the work of sculptor John Hughes) was removed. It languished in storage until it was shipped to Australia and unveiled in Sydney in 1987.

Thus Victoria had a relatively smooth passage, but Nelson's Pillar in Dublin came to a peculiar if predictable end. Here a 13-foot statue of Admiral Nelson surmounted a great granite Doric column, making a total height of 134 feet. It was erected in 1809 to commemorate the hero of Trafalgar and was located in the middle of what was then Sackville (now O'Connell) Street. Nelson's Pillar dominated the street and was seen as representing the true heart of Dublin. 'Meet you at the pillar' was a usual arrangement to make an appointment. However, after Irish independence there was much controversy and unease at the central position of an English hero who really had nothing to do with Ireland or Dublin. Matters came to a head in 1966, the 50th anniversary of the 1916 Easter Rising. One night in March of that year, a maverick section of the outlawed IRA blew off the top half of the pillar. Deemed unsafe, the remaining stump was removed by Irish Army engineers over a week later. It was Dublin's loss. The pillar, if not the particular statue, offered a proportional and pleasing counterpoint in the centre of the city. It was finally replaced in 2003 by the pin-like Monument of Light. This is also known as the Spire, all 398 stainless-steel feet of it. In turn this has been controversial. Many feel it lacks any great aesthetic merit, is more suited to a provincial city and does not add lustre to a European capital. Dubliners with their wry and iconoclastic wit have given it the dubious nickname of 'the stiffy in the Liffey'.

DUBLIN, PALM TREES AND THE DUCAL STABLES
1817

The Wellington Testimonial, an obelisk erected in tribute to the eponymous Duke, is a fine sight to behold in Dublin's great Phoenix Park, the largest urban park in Europe. At 67 yards high of pointed granite, it is reputedly also the highest obelisk in Europe. It was paid for by subscription from the great and the good of Dublin. Funds were short and it took 44 years to complete, being finally unveiled in 1861. Carefully venture up the sloping steps to the base of the plinth. Set around the sides are plaques made of bronze cast from cannons captured from the French at Waterloo. On the northern side is a long rectangular plaque that denotes the Siege of Seringapatam. The panoramic scene shows striving soldiers, expertly directed by an officer, others manning a cannon, with palm trees in the background.

Hang on a minute! Seringawhat? Isn't this a trifle rare and unusual for this bucolic part of Dublin, this huge park with its green sward, deer and deciduous trees (but no tropical palm trees) as far as the eye can see? Well, the answer lies many thousands of miles away. The famous victory at Seringapatam was a seminal event in the expansion of the British East India Company to extend its control south across the subcontinent. The pesky Sultan of Mysore, Tippu Sultan, had inconsiderately been resisting the expansion of the Company into his domain! He also had the impudence to defeat British forces over previous decades. So it was that the young Arthur Wesley, the future duke, now a colonel with the 33rd Regiment, found himself stationed in India. Fortuitously his brother, Richard, Lord Mornington, was now appointed as Governor-General of India. It was at this time that the family decided to change their name to the grander 'Wellesley'.

When the conflict broke out with Tippu Sultan in 1799, a large British force headed south and fought their way towards the Sultan's headquarters at Seringapatam. This was a city surrounded by large fortifications on an island by the River Cauvery, around 10 miles north of Mysore. Wellesley fought bravely in the fierce battle. Eventually, the British forces stormed in through a breach in the walls and captured the city. Tippu died in the battle. The event was a seminal one and as a consequence the British were able to take over the south of India – an important basis for the future creation of the British Raj. Wellesley was made Governor of Seringapatam and Mysore and was promoted to brigadier general. While there, he lived in Tippu Sultan's Summer Palace for several years. The airy palace, made of timber and decorated with fantastical murals, can still be seen today.

On leaving India in 1804, Wellesley's career went into overdrive, with each new achievement capping the previous one. He fought in the Peninsular Campaign against Napoleon in Spain and Portugal, being appointed commander in 1809 and successfully fighting his way across the peninsula. On his entry to Madrid in 1812, he was honoured by a portrait made by none other than Goya. Returning to Britain as an all-conquering hero, he was created the Duke of Wellington. His finest hour came after Napoleon escaped from Elba in 1815 and regained control of France. Most likely, the people in Britain, would now be speaking French had the Duke got it wrong at the Battle of Waterloo. He expertly presided over the allied forces at the decisive battle near Brussels that finally put an end to the perceived Napoleonic menace. How does one follow a famous victory like that? Why, by becoming Prime Minister! He resigned as Commander-in-Chief, entered politics and was Prime Minister from 1828 to 1830 (and again very briefly in 1834). Later, he spent his days as the grand old man of the realm and died in 1852.

So, commemorating Wellington in Dublin makes sense, including those exotic battles in faraway places. After all, he was born there. On 1 May 1769 Arthur Wesley was born at No. 6 Merrion Street in the city. He was the child of Lord and Lady Mornington, landowners of Trim, Co. Meath, and was baptised in St Kevin's Church, Camden Row (the church is now in ruins and the baptismal font can be found in the church in Taney, Co. Dublin).

He was sent to Eton, but was not successful there and he was then enrolled in the French Royal Academy of Equitation. Horsemanship, French and knowledge of the European continent – all of these were to stand him in good stead later on. In 1787 he enlisted in the British Army. With not a little influence, he was appointed aide-de-camp to the Lord Lieutenant of Ireland. Now a lieutenant, he enjoyed the social whirl of balls and levees in Dublin Castle. In those days one could 'double-job' and he was able to combine his military career with being elected a Member of Parliament for Trim in the Irish House of Commons in College Green.

So, this was one son of Dublin who, during his early years, was pretty well intertwined with the city. One might think that he would harbour nostalgia about Dublin and Ireland, especially after they built him such an impressive monument. The rather surprising thing is that the steely-minded Duke harboured an aversion to his native city and country. It may date from his time at Eton, where some say that he was teased about his Anglo-Irish background. The following quotation has been attributed to the Duke himself, but in reality it was the Irish nationalist leader Daniel O'Connell who, in a speech of 1844, said of him: 'The poor old Duke! What shall I say of him? To be sure he was born in Ireland, but being born in a stable does not make a man a horse.'

MAKING CONNECTIONS:
AN ILLUMINATING STORY
OF GREAT GAS
1820

Merrion Square in central Dublin is bounded by terraces of fine Georgian houses, with their famous elegant and colourful door fronts. Walk into the fine city park at the heart of the square. There you can experience pleasant walks, green swards and see many interesting statues. As you walk around, you will notice a curious thing; all the lampposts seem to be different. And they are. Dublin City Council has cleverly collected and installed here its historic collection of these essential pieces of street furniture. Those on display range from the original gas lamps, through all the gradations of the electric age. If you ever go to see this, enter by the eastern entrance of the square, where there's a good map that denotes the various types of lamppost.

The night was dangerous in the cities of hundreds of years ago. Footpads and other malefactors would lurk, exulting in the freedom the dark granted to go about their lucrative trades. Street lighting became an essential for public order in the cities. In Dublin, as gas street lights replaced oil lamps during the 1820s, three gas companies emerged. One of these was the Dublin Oil Gas Company, of Great Brunswick (now Pearse) Street. The premises of this gas company is still there, becoming the Antient Concert Rooms in the Victorian era, then a cinema. Now it houses offices. In the early days gas was produced from whale oil. Fleets of whaling ships set out to secure this oil for the world. It is easy to see why Herman Melville in *Moby Dick* describes whale oil as being 'as rare as the milk of queens'.

The utility business has always had hints of being a tough trade, of being raw in tooth and claw. Look at the behaviour of the present-day oil and gas companies, not to mind your inflated water and gas bills issued by our esteemed utility companies! These dodgy characteristics have been finessed over time and have a long heritage. In the Dublin of the early 19th century there was something of the Wild West about the gas business. The three gas companies in the city were in strong competition with each other, as gas lighting and heating began to be used in houses. Sometimes their respective pipes were laid in parallel along the same street. Tales, perhaps apocryphal, recount that it was a common practice in the gas companies to pay clandestine bonuses to foremen. This was in recognition of their services, which included the ability to quietly connect customers to a rival gas line, while their company continued to bill them.

IN ROLLICKING GOOD HUMOUR: THE SUCCESSFUL VISIT OF GEORGE IV

1821

Over in the Kingdom of Ireland, there was upheaval in 1798 when a rebellion broke out. It was put down bloodily, but not before 30,000 people had perished. Fearful of further disturbance, the Irish Parliament in Dublin was induced (by not a little bribery) to vote itself out of existence and move to London, as marked by the Act of Union passed in 1800. This was the background to King George IV's visit to Dublin in 1821, the first visit to Ireland by a British monarch since 1690 when William of Orange (William III) enjoyed his decisive victory at the Battle of the Boyne.

George IV, of the Hanoverian dynasty, had been Regent during the last years of his father, mad King George III. By the time he came to the throne in 1820 at the age of 57, he had incurred massive debts, was obese and had a string of mistresses and illegitimate children.

Normally visits by royalty were rather staid affairs. However, the peculiar thing was that when George IV landed in Howth, a harbour five miles to the north of Dublin, on 12 August 1821, he was drunk, having consumed goose pie and (appropriately) Irish whiskey punch. He was in good humour, having heard the news of the death five days before of his estranged wife, Princess Caroline of Brunswick. Incidentally, steps have been carved into the stone quayside where the King first trod, and can still be seen today.

Dubliners had always harboured a fondness for royalty. One account related that the news of the King's impending visit 'threw the people of Dublin into a paroxysm of joy'. In Dublin preparations were under way, not least a dinner at Morrison's Hotel (at two guineas a head) of 400 prominent citizens, with 15 hogsheads of porter (a type of brown malt beer) being laid on to drink to the King's good health.

George headed to the Vice-regal Lodge in the Phoenix Park, where he rested over the following days. On 17 August he made his triumphal progress to the centre of the city. The principal thoroughfare, Sackville Street, had been decked with garlands and triumphal arches and the royal pendant flew from the Nelson Pillar. Fireworks were set off and an artillery salute boomed by the partly constructed Wellington Testimonial as the King left the Phoenix Park. A roar came from the huge crowd lining Sackville Street as he came into view, along with a shout of 'God save the King'. After ceremonies there with many dignitaries he moved on to receive a formal welcome at Dublin Castle. Several days of levees, dinners and celebrations followed.

Finally, everybody needed a break. So it was that on 24 August, his formal duties over, the King set off rather rapidly to Slane Castle (over 30 miles to the north of Dublin), seat of the Marquis of Conyngham. There, the new widower was consoled by the good Lady Conyngham, a royal mistress of long standing.

He left Ireland on 3 September from the great harbour at Dunleary, which was renamed Kingstown (since renamed Dún Laoghaire) in honour of his visit. George IV's visit was deemed a great success. The Lord Mayor of Dublin in a final address at the quayside said that the King 'had vanquished every bad passion in six millions of the Irish people'.

MEASURING OVER LAND AND MOUNTAIN: MR EVEREST COMES TO DUBLIN AND INSPECTS ITS BARS
1824

In 1824 it was proposed to establish an Ordnance Survey to map Ireland. Mapping countries is undertaken for many reasons. One is the military rationale that accurate maps make it easier to control territory. The other reason is financial: a proper map is required to better plan the taxation of a country. The Duke of Wellington, the Master General of Ordnance at the time, ordered the establishment of the survey. Although born in Dublin, he was scathing about the local talent: 'I positively refuse to employ any surveyor in Ireland upon this service.' And so it was that the Irish Ordnance Survey was initially staffed entirely by British sappers. Work commenced in 1825 with the headquarters located in the Phoenix Park in Dublin.

The basis of a survey is triangulation, first establishing a long baseline, then measuring angles from the ends of this to prominent points to allow calculations of distances. In using these techniques, the Irish survey was pioneering in many ways. Mountains were frequently covered in fog and difficult to see. Limelight, an intense light already in use in theatres, was positioned on mountain tops, to enable measurements to be taken over long distances. Also, the survey in Ireland was undertaken at a six-inch scale to the mile, as opposed to the one-inch scale previously used in Britain. To achieve such a large scale required special accuracy. The basis of any survey is the baseline. If that is not accurate, the whole survey, both distances and heights, will be out of kilter. Previously measurements had been made using chains. In the course of the Irish survey, more accurate devices known as Compensation Bars were developed. Brass and iron bars were used in an arrangement that cancelled out temperature effects, and allowed incredibly precise measurement of the baseline length.

Continents away, a massive topographical project, the Great Triangulation Survey of India, was under way. The centre of this was the great spine 1,600 miles long, known as the 'Great Arc of India'. It was the largest meridian arc to be calculated anywhere in the world. The superintendent of the survey, George Everest, was an energetic man, eager to discover improved methods and instruments to use for his survey. While on extended home leave he paid a three-month visit to the Ordnance Survey in the Phoenix Park in 1829, staying as a house guest in Dublin of William Rowan Hamilton (see page 68 and 74-75), mathematical genius and enthusiast in all matters relating to surveys and trigonometry.

In Dublin, Everest had an opportunity to inspect the Ordnance Survey and its advanced techniques. On his departure, he resolved to increase his staff levels in India to something similar to those pertaining in Dublin. Crucially, he also obtained two sets of Compensation Bars, all the better to ensure accurate baselines for the great survey under way in the subcontinent. He returned to his Great Arc in 1830 and was appointed Surveyor-General of India.

As the Indian survey progressed, they continued through British India and eventually reached the northern frontier with Nepal. At the time this was a closed kingdom and it was not possible to cross the border and continue to survey. From this frontier, the surveyors, looking through their large brass theodolites, mapped the enormous range of snow-capped mountains of the great Himalayas that extended to the North. The mountains were spectacularly high but one, they established, was the highest in the world. Thus in 1856, with exceptional accuracy and using the instruments of the time, they calculated that this great mountain, over 100 miles away, was 29,002ft high. This was only 27 feet out in comparison with today's calculation. In 1865, it was decided to name the mountain after (the by now Sir) George Everest. It is a charming and beguiling fact that part of the basis of the exceptional accuracy of measuring the world's highest mountain can be put down, even if in a small way, to the sophistication of the Ordnance Survey in Dublin, its Compensation Bars and the knowledge that Sir George Everest garnered there.

HOUGHTON'S DROP
1830

Located within Phoenix Park, Dublin Zoo was founded in 1830. It is the world's third oldest public zoo, as it opened just after those in Paris and London. This new institution fitted squarely with the contemporary hunger for science, knowledge and improvement. It also helped that the British Empire was expanding, with access to yet more strange lands and exotic creatures. The zoo today has many fine refurbished Victorian buildings. Noteworthy are the original thatched entrance lodge, the Roberts House and the timber loggia of the (splendidly renovated) Haughton Memorial Building.

Dubliners have always had an affinity for what they call the 'Ah-zoo'. In 1831 there were only five species on display: two ostriches from Africa, one sambar deer from India, two wapiti deer, two emus from Australia and two passenger pigeons from America. From these small beginnings of less than two hectares, it has expanded greatly to 28 hectares, benefiting from the large amount of space available within the park. This now affords an opportunity to see a huge range of wild animals.

Using the latest concepts in zoo management, many animals can be observed in naturalistic spaces with vegetation and water features reflecting their native habitats. Being in natural social groups, they are able to breed and raise their own young. For example, animals of African origin are free to roam in the African Plains area, which covers 13 hectares.

There is a possible and surprising connection between the plains of Dublin Zoo and the wide open spaces of Hollywood in California. From 1855, when it acquired its first lion, Dublin Zoo gained an international reputation for expertise in breeding lions. 'Cairbre', born in Dublin in 1927, is reputed to have been one of the lions (many different ones were used) that roared in the title sequence at the beginning of the MGM movies. One does not know if it roared in a Dublin accent.

The Haughton Memorial Building is named after one of the early guiding lights of the zoo, Samuel Haughton. He was a leading member of the Zoological Society and served as president in the 1860s. Haughton was a brilliant scholar, having three doctorates and a medical degree. He was Professor of Geography at Trinity College and President of the Royal Irish Academy. He calculated the age of the earth as 2,300 million years. That was pretty close for his era, as current estimates are at around 4,500 million years.

However, it was in the macabre area of hanging that this genteel clergyman and scientist pushed the boundaries of practical science. Previously the hangman would have to guess how much rope to use in each case: an excessive length could decapitate a condemned person; too short and they would endure a slow strangulation. Haughton was conscious of these barbarities and worked to establish a more humane method, developing a mathematical table that became known as 'Haughton's Drop', which became standard practice in the 1870s. It allowed calculation of the correct drop to ensure instantaneous breaking of the neck, resulting in a swift death.

OF DUBLIN EXTRACTION: THE GLASNEVIN RESURRECTIONISTS

1832

Ireland has always had a strong medical tradition. There was a large proportion of Irish surgeons in the British Army during the Napoleonic Wars. The provision of doctors accentuated the need to provide medical training; hence there were numerous medical schools in Dublin. In the British and Irish medical arena, however, there was a darker tradition. The law allowed only the bodies of executed criminals to be used for dissection; hence there was an insufficient number of bodies available to meet the need for teaching anatomy. In response to the demand, the profession of body-snatchers (or resurrectionists) arose to shoulder the burden. Many will know the story of Burke and Hare in Edinburgh. These Irish immigrants did not bother to dig up graves. They chose a more direct (should one say, fresher) route. In order to meet the high demand for corpses, they simply went and murdered their victims, 17 in all.

Back to Dublin, where demand for fresh bodies was high. In addition to the requirements of the local medical schools, there were the needs of those in Edinburgh and London to be catered for; £40 per corpse was the rather handsome price that prevailed for this export trade. Faced with a plague of grave robberies in Dublin at the beginning of the 19th century, the graves of the newly interred were surrounded by large and solid cages of wrought iron, known as 'mortsafes'.

Glasnevin Cemetery is now the principal cemetery of Dublin and dates from 1832. It had its origins when Daniel O'Connell's Catholic Association bought nine acres at Glasnevin, on the northern outskirts of the city. The avowed objective was to bury 'people of all religions and none' with dignity. Five large castellated watchtowers were built at the corners of the high walls that encircled the cemetery, so that a lookout could be kept for the nocturnal body-snatchers. The pressure eased off as changes in the law eventually allowed a more liberal supply of bodies for medical schools. However, as late as 1853, a pack of Cuban bloodhounds was on patrol in Glasnevin to deter this macabre trade.

If macabre is your thing, you may inspect a full-size display of the technique of body-snatching in the sparkling new museum (one of the few museums in the world to be found in a cemetery) recently opened at Glasnevin Cemetery, now calling itself 'Ireland's necropolis'. There you descend into the aptly named section in the basement called 'The City of the Dead'. Among the exhibits you can see a tableau that depicts how the crafty exponent of this black art was able to create a narrow tunnel directly to the head of the coffin, send a hook down and neatly extract the body.

FROM PERISCOPES TO IPHONES
1833

The suburb of Rathmines in Dublin (see pages 99–100 and 118–119) is not a place normally associated with advanced manufacturing, optics or physics. Yet this once-genteel suburb was home to cutting-edge technology in those fields. The Grubb Optical and Mechanical Works were located here. It had been founded by Thomas Grubb, who had commenced his career by making engraving machines that could print numbered banknotes for the Bank of Ireland. The company made clocks and then, with the founding of the Grubb Telescope Company in 1833, developed mastery in the intricate instrumentation of telescopes and the grinding of lenses. In due course Thomas's son, Howard Grubb, who trained as a civil engineer at Trinity College, took over the helm. Under his direction, large sophisticated telescopes were developed and manufactured in Rathmines. These were exported to observatories in Europe, Australia and South Africa. In 1875 the firm secured a contract to supply a 27-inch telescope for Vienna, making it at the time the largest refracting telescope in the world. Howard Grubb was knighted by Queen Victoria in 1887. Working examples of Grubb instruments can still be seen, including the South telescope at Dunsink observatory near Dublin.

The naval arms race between Britain and its rapidly industrialising rival, Germany, gathered pace at the start of the 20th century and resulted in new business for the company. The Grubb firm went on to supply 95 per cent of the periscopes for British submarines during the First World War. After the 1916 Rising in Dublin, the British Admiralty, worried about security of supply, insisted that production no longer be carried out in Dublin. Rathmines works closed in 1920.

Fast forward to today; most people have a mobile phone, or even an iPad. These devices have a clock, controlled by radio waves, with a connection to the Internet. The surprising thing is that the first coherent proposal for a radio-controlled clock was made by Sir Howard Grubb in 1898, in a talk given to the Royal Dublin Society. 'There is something very beautiful in this action of the "Marconi" wave … setting each clock … absolutely right,' he said. 'We might go even still further … to carry an apparatus in one's pocket and have our watches automatically set by this electrical wave as we walk about the street.' This Dublin genius thus predicted the radio-controlled watch around 90 years before the first one appeared.

COMPENSATING LORD CLONCURRY

1834

The Scottish engineer John Rennie began development of the great harbour at Dunleary to the south of Dublin in 1817. The silting up of Dublin port gave impetus to the idea of running a ship canal from the city to connect with this new harbour. However, the benefits of that new invention, the railway, were becoming evident. The great and the good of Dublin duly came together to plan one and the Dublin and Kingstown Railway Act received Royal Assent in 1831.

Charles Blacker Vignoles was engaged as chief engineer for the project. Vignoles, born in County Wexford, was a veteran of the pioneering Liverpool and Manchester Railway. He later had a stellar career designing railways through the mountains of northern Spain, as well as a large-span chain bridge over the Dnieper at Kiev in what was then Tsarist Russia. He also developed the flat-bottomed rail, the classic rail now in use all over the world.

The contractor William Dargan began laying the railway along the coast of the Irish Sea. Great sea embankments were constructed, some of parabolic shape, to repel the waves. Masons laboured to erect a series of granite bridges for the elevated line, high above the city streets, heading out of the Westland Row terminus. Granite blocks were carved to support the wrought-iron T-shaped rails, and work proceeded at a great pace on the railway, which had a length of over five miles. Alas, a major flood on the River Dodder swept away the railway bridge at the Dublin suburb of Ballsbridge two months before the planned opening date, causing a temporary timber structure to hastily be built. So it was that on 17 December 1834, the steam locomotive Hibernia set out with a first-class carriage (a first-class ticket costing 1s), three second-class carriages, and four of third class. The locomotive hauled around 5,000 passengers between Dublin and Kingstown in the course of the day; it was the first suburban railway in the world.

Floods, great embankments, sea barriers or no, the greatest obstacle to completion of the railway was the obdurate objections of two important landowners. The railway had to pass through the coastal lands in south Dublin at Monkstown of Lord Cloncurry (where he had 'Maretimo', his summer residence) and his neighbour, Sir Harcourt Lees. These men were hugely influential and were able to say no in several ways with great authority. Vignoles set off to persuade the two gentlemen of the benefits of the railway. He brought with him plans and models and eventually persuaded them that he could conceal the railway from their residences. However, the aristocratic gentlemen drove a hard bargain. Sir Harcourt Lees got £7,500 and a bridge. Lord Cloncurry settled for the lesser £3,000, but he received something much more costly: a cutting through a hill, plus a private footbridge (with classical piers in severe granite) over the railway line to facilitate access to the seashore. The railway also had to construct for him a boat-slip and a pier together with a bathing lodge in the shape of a Grecian temple.

The strange thing is that Lord Cloncurry was very experienced when it came to compensation. Many years before, in 1807, he had taken the well-known rake, Sir John Piers, to court for 'criminal conversation' with his wife. The affair came to light when Piers had been observed acting in a 'preoccupied' manner with (the new and very young) Lady Cloncurry at Lyons Estate, Cloncurry's main residence, in County Kildare, to the west of Dublin. This was in the same room as the Italian painter Gaspar Gabrielli, who happened to be perched on a ladder at work on a mural at the time. Cloncurry was awarded the enormous sum of £20,000 in damages, and Sir John Piers was ruined. The sum was nearly seven times more than Cloncurry was able to extract from the railway, 27 years later.

John Betjeman immortalised the story of Lady Cloncurry's disgrace in a poem entitled 'The Fête Champêtre', which starts off with a boating party on a lake:

And a boatload of beauty darts over the tide,
The Baron Cloncurry and also his bride.

   ...

But why has the Lady Cloncurry such fears?
Oh, one of the guests will be Baronet Piers.

MOUNT JEROME AND THE SPRING-LOADED PORTAL TO HEAVEN

1836

During the 19th century, most of the Dublin haute-bourgeoisie lived in the southern suburbs. What better arrangement to accommodate them after their demise than a fine spacious cemetery, conveniently located within a hearse's horse-clop of the beckoning suburbs? Mount Jerome opened for business in 1836, located in Harold's Cross near the burgeoning middle-class suburbs, south of the Grand Canal. As you enter the cemetery you see that it is graced by a fine funerary chapel, built in 1847. This was the first Gothic church in Dublin that was in full conformity with the Victorian architect A.W. Pugin's principles of Gothic Revival. Walk further and you see, extending all over, the great memorials to posterity, testimony to the self-aggrandisement of the Victorian middle classes. This is one of the great atmospheric 19th-century cemeteries, on a par with Père Lachaise in Paris and Highgate in London, albeit on a smaller scale.

Here are the graves of Dublin's Victorian merchant princes, professional men, scholars, soldiers and artists. Buried here, among others, are Sheridan le Fanu (writer of Gothic novels, including one on lesbian vampires!), William Rowan Hamilton and the progenitors of some of Dublin's literary titans: Oscar Wilde's father (see pages 88–89) as well as Bram Stoker's. A more recent resident is the Dublin criminal known as the 'General' (see pages 139–140).

The century-old atmosphere of Mount Jerome is spoilt by the somewhat breathless enviro-speak on the cemetery company's website: it is 'the most environmentally friendly Irish crematorium'; their 'carbon footprint has been reduced by 30%.' They are also rather proud of their 'automatic coffin loading system'.

It is still worth a wander around the older part of the cemetery. The Victorians took death seriously; the more important you were in life, the grander your memorial. Here are Greco-Roman temples, angels, urns and much more. Step down to the passages below ground level, with their terraced vaults. The great cast-iron doors, now covered with red rust, still protect their noble and permanent occupants. Some still have nameplates in ornate 19th-century lettering.

It is all rather poignant and, if one can say this about a graveyard, delightful. For a touch of the strange and unexpected, stroll along a central walkway and look at two tombs in particular. On one, the Harvie memorial, the figure of a grieving dog is on top of the great rectangular granite tomb, standing on a cloak. He is howling to the heavens, lamenting his master who died by drowning. Later, when the dog died, it was interred here with its master. A short distance away, against a background of trees, is the Gresham tomb. This is a large pyramid-style monument with a flat top, again constructed in granite. The solid cast-iron door has the family name, with a plaque of the family coat of arms carved in the granite above. The construction of this tomb was based on an extraordinary premise. The lady, who was buried within, had a horror of being buried alive. Consequently there is a chain from the coffin to a bell at the top of the tomb, which would have allowed the occupant to ring for assistance in the felicitous chance that she woke up. As an added precaution against her being buried alive, the coffin had a spring-loaded arrangement that could be released from within.

THE FASTEST MAN IN THE VICTORIAN WORLD
1843

Nature abhors a vacuum. The people of the growing township of Dalkey wanted a connection to the port of Kingstown (Dún Laoghaire) just under two miles away. However, putting in a new-fangled steam-powered railway would present a problem: the terrain was of solid granite and the burghers of Kingstown objected to their seafront being obscured by trains. Over in England in 1839 a patent had been granted for a new form of locomotion, one that employed a vacuum in a cylinder to create the propulsive force. And no steam locomotive with a high smoke stack was required.

So, the Dublin and Kingstown Railway commenced to build an atmospheric railway along an old tramway line, previously used to transport granite from Dalkey Quarry for construction of the great harbour at Kingstown. A relatively shallow cutting was excavated so the new railway would be out of sight. A 15-inch cast-iron cylinder was located between the rails and a waxed leather flap valve was arranged along the top of the pipe. A steam-powered pumping station in Dalkey pumped to extract the air and maintain a vacuum in the pipe (fittingly the road where it was located is now called Atmospheric Road). A piston in the pipe was connected by a rod to the leading carriage and this vacuum propelled the carriages up the incline towards Dalkey. Gravity was the propulsion for the return journey. The line opened in March 1844, being the first commercial atmospheric railway in the world. Trains ran every half an hour and at peak times up to nine carriages were used.

However, one day during the testing phase in 1843 an extraordinary event occurred that would have featured in the 1843 *Guinness World Records*, it if had been in existence then! A young engineering student, as part of the test regime, sat in the leading carriage. Unbeknown to him, it was not connected to the other carriages. The pumping station in Dalkey steamed up and created the vacuum. Suddenly, the carriage with the young student shot uphill like a rocket. The speed increased and by the time it reached Dalkey Station it had reached the unheard of speed of 84mph, truly a world speed record, albeit an undesired one. The unfortunate young man staggered out of the carriage in a state of shock.

There is an apocryphal story that the atmospheric system failed because rats continually ate the waxed leather flaps. In reality the steam pumping station was prone to breakdown. Passenger traffic had also dropped off due to the great Irish Famine. By 1854, the railway company had had enough and decided to install a conventional steam railway, deepening the cutting further and installing track to the new Irish gauge of 5ft 3in. Flower-bed bridges were installed over the line to obscure the cutting and some of these are still in place today, as the Dublin Area Rapid Transit (DART) electric trains sweep along below.

INCHING TOWARDS A
JUDGEMENT OF SOLOMON
1843

Lack of joined-up thinking is a serious matter when it comes to track gauge. This is the distance between the two rails of a railway track. It usually makes sense to have the same gauge if you want to run trains on the same section of line!

In the early Victorian era Ireland, no less than Britain, was experiencing a railway boom. This was all exciting and new, with the sweet smell of progress. Railways were seen as the panacea for all kinds of social and economic problems. 'Projectors', as railway promoters were called, were coming up with plans for a web of railways criss-crossing Ireland. In those febrile times, railway technology was not settled, not least the width of the track gauge.

Dublin was where the problem came to light. Construction had begun on a new railway line heading north from the city to Drogheda. In 1843, the directors of the railway decided that a gauge of 5ft 2in was the best for them and this would be used. However, the new Ulster Railway, heading south out of Belfast, had just been laid at a gauge of 6ft 2in. The penny dropped: it was going to be difficult to connect up a future Dublin to Belfast railway line. A further complication was that the pioneering Dublin and Kingstown railway of nine years earlier, to the south of Dublin, had been laid at a gauge of 4ft 8½in.

Three track gauges in prospect – so what to do? As all governments do in times of doubt, they called in an expert. The Board of Trade assigned Major General Pasley to look into the matter. He consulted widely and met with the leading railway practitioners in Britain (where, in a similar fashion, there were vastly differing railway gauges in use). Two particular gauges were among those under general consideration: those of 5ft and 5ft 6in (as it happened, these gauges were chosen for, respectively, Russian railways and Indian railways). The Major General split the difference and, having satisfied himself that this would work, he proposed the gauge of 5ft 3in. That became the Irish gauge, and trains today run on this in the Republic and in Northern Ireland. What is now called standard gauge (4ft 8½in) was chosen in Britain – how it came to be in use across the world is another story.

Back to the lines radiating out of Dublin, now being laid to 5ft 3in. So far, so insular. However, the strange thing is that the Irish gauge is also in use on thousands of miles of track elsewhere in the world, much larger in total than the Irish network. It was adopted in Brazil for a series of railways, the first of which was inaugurated in 1867. Equally, large sections of track in Australia are laid to Irish gauge. This was introduced by a 19th-century Irish railway engineer, Francis Webb Shields, who chose what he knew best. Curiously, the Irish gauge was also used in New Zealand for its first railway in 1863. Fourteen years later it was decided to adopt a uniform 3ft 6in gauge for all railways. The locomotives and wagons (to Irish gauge), now surplus, were sold to Australian railways. Much of this equipment was lost when the ship transporting them was wrecked.

INTO ORBIT:
QUATERNIONS ON
BROUGHAM BRIDGE
1843

It is commonplace today to hear of spacecraft navigating their way through the heavens. Even more commonplace are the graphics used to interface with a computer, iPad or phone. It may take a while to comprehend that this advanced technology has a link with an event that occurred over 160 years ago at a canal bridge located in what is now a run-down outskirt of Dublin.

The mathematical genius William Rowan Hamilton was born in Dublin in 1805. An infant prodigy, at the age of 12 he compiled a grammar in the obscure language of Syriac. He was appointed Astronomer Royal of Ireland and Professor of Astronomy at Trinity College Dublin when only 21 and still an undergraduate. Hamilton, polymath that he was, was rather disorganised. He did not devote much of his time to practical astronomy at the observatory at Dunsink in north Dublin, but spent many hours in a reverie, pondering scientific matters. His study was strewn with a large mass of papers. Once, contemplating mathematical relationships in the shade of a haycock, when asked what he had been thinking, he replied that he was trying to 'multiply the North-East by the South-East'. Thus, he spent much of his time assaulting the limits of known science across a wide front.

He discovered conical refraction, and carried out work on dynamics and many other mathematical formulae. Hamilton was not a mere scientist: he appreciated and wrote poetry too. William Wordsworth developed a friendship with him, becoming his poetical mentor and visiting him at Dunsink on three occasions. Hamilton, knighted in 1835, was recognised as the first foreign associate of the newly founded United States National Academy of Sciences just before he died in 1865.

But the event that concerns us here is 16 October 1843, which proved to be a seminal day. A stroll along the towpath of the Royal Canal was to prove inspirational and would result in a ground-breaking concept that has implications for us all today. Sir William was walking with his wife by the quiet waters of the canal, not far from Dunsink. Passing by the fine cut-stone arched Brougham Bridge he had a Eureka moment, and the theory of quaternions suddenly came to him. Using his pen-knife, he inscribed the formula '$i^2 = j^2 = k^2 = ijk = -1$' on the wall of the bridge.

In the latter part of the 20th century quaternions came to be recognised as of fundamental importance in fields such as physics, computer simulations and electrical engineering, and are now used as a basis of all aspects of electronics.

QUEEN VICTORIA'S VISITS TO DUBLIN: LEVEES AND THE HIGH THRONE

1849

> Queen Vic she came to call on us,
> She wanted to meet all of us –
> 'Tis well she did not fall on us, she's 18 stone

Thus runs a rather ribald Dublin song called 'Monto' (see pages 130–1). Queen Victoria came to visit the city on four occasions. The first time, in 1849, was deemed a great success. She was a young woman and accompanied by her consort, Prince Albert. Never fully at ease in Ireland, the Queen found it a trifle strange and sometimes burdensome. She later wrote that the Lord Mayor presented her with the keys of the city, 'with some appropriate words, spoken in an amazing brogue'. She went to Dublin Castle and there received the great and the good at a three-hour levee. Even though the legs of the throne in the Throne Room, installed for a previous visit by George IV, had been hastily cut in anticipation of her visit, she noted later that 'I sat myself on the throne, the seat of which was so high that I had difficulty in sitting on it … It [the levee] was hard work and the people were awkward and some ridiculous.' After her visit she ennobled the Lord Mayor and appointed her son, the Prince of Wales, aged eight, as Earl of Dublin.

The 1853 Exhibition of Industry and Arts in Dublin (inspired by the 1851 Crystal Palace Exhibition in London) was the next occasion of a royal visit, during which the Queen took a great interest in the exhibition, visiting three times. There she purchased the Irish State Coach, made by the Dublin coach-building firm of Hutton's, a coach still used in London by the monarch at the State Opening of Parliament. The organiser of the exhibition was William Dargan, a successful contractor who built railways across Ireland. He is now remembered as 'the father of Irish railways'. Dargan represented her Majesty's ideal Irishman: vigorous and enterprising. She visited him at his home at Mount Anville in Dublin's southern suburbs and offered a baronetcy, an honour that he declined.

The Queen and Prince Albert paid another visit in the summer of 1861 to see the Prince of Wales, who had just commenced his military training at the Curragh in County Kildare, just to the West of Dublin (see pages 83–4 for more details of his escapades there). Later that year, in December, Prince Albert died. The Queen was grief-stricken and withdrew from public duties. It cast a pall on her reign that was not to lift for more than 20 years. In 1862, a committee was set up in Dublin with the purpose of erecting a statue to the deceased prince. St Stephen's Green was under consideration for the location of the statue, as well as a proposal that it be renamed Albert Park. This proposal was not approved.

It has been speculated that this was one of the reasons that Queen Victoria did not visit Dublin, or indeed Ireland, for 39 years after the visit in 1861. She came in April 1900 in the last year of her life. Ostensibly this was to give thanks to the troops from Ireland who had participated in the Boer War. Nationalists sourly said that it was to encourage further recruitment to the British Army for the war, still being waged. The curious thing was that, after such a long absence, she visited for so long, three weeks this time, staying in the Vice-regal Lodge in the Phoenix Park. Despite being frail, over the following weeks she clattered in her carriage all over the city, meeting the worthy and the deserving. There were levees and parades as well as a great reception for children in the Phoenix Park. The welcome for her was overwhelming and extensive.

This visit was also perceived as a success. With the hurrahs resounding in her ears, she left on the Royal Yacht, little realising that there was to be a cataclysmic rebellion in Dublin against the Empire a mere 16 years later.

THE RICH ARE DIFFERENT: BALLS, CUES AND MONKEYS

1853

The Victorian era was an excellent time to be an architect. It was a time of prosperity and progress as the fruits of the industrial revolution became available. New architectural commissions abounded for factories, banks, villas, colleges and (as there was more to life than mere Mammon!) churches. So it was in Dublin in the 19th century. There wasn't much by way of industrial buildings, but as the city expanded as a financial, administrative and commercial centre, there was a need for grandiose banks, insurance offices and other institutional buildings.

There were many eminent architects practising in the city during that time. Prominent were Sir Thomas Deane and Benjamin Woodward. One of their outstanding works is the Museum Building in Trinity College which dates from 1853–57. Externally this grey limestone building could be considered to have similarities with a grand Venetian palazzo. The great entrance hall within is a tour de force, its two grand domes have echoes of the Hagia Sofia, the remarkable church of Byzantine Constantinople. Both within and without exquisite stone carvings can be seen. The architects used an ensemble of stone carvers, among them the talented O'Shea brothers from Cork. These carvers also worked with Deane and Woodward for their acclaimed Oxford University Museum of Natural History (1860). Just a long cricket ball's flight away from the Museum Building, over the adjacent Trinity cricket pitch, is another masterpiece by the architectural duo. This is the Kildare Street Club (1859–61), located on the eponymous street. It is a fine building, in the Italianate style, blended with Byzantine. This red-brick building also contains sublime stone carving.

During Dublin's great Georgian period, the lords who came to attend Parliament travelled from their country estates to stay in the city where they had purchased great terraced town houses, set in the grand squares. However, the Irish Parliament moved to London after the Act of Union in 1800, and so too did the lords. Things changed in Dublin during the Victorian era. Institutions like the Kildare Street Club provided a place to stay in the city for rich (male) landowners. It also afforded congenial leisure and dining facilities for the local haute-bourgeoisie.

Many observers cast a sceptical eye on these rich people within their gilded domain. In 1886, the novelist George Moore wrote scathingly of the Kildare Street Club and its members. He commented on how they spent their days drinking sherry and that they had an 'oyster-like capacity ... [so] that they should continue to get fat in the bed that they are born. This club is a sort of oyster-bed into which all the eldest sons of the landed gentry fall as a matter of course.'

Look at the Kildare Street Club building today and you see that it is decorated with a series of stone carvings, on the bases of the external columns both at first- and ground-floor levels. These depict a fantastical series of animals, from a hound chasing a hare to an animal playing a lute. The most original and curious carving can be seen on the ground floor, just to the right of the entrance (of what is now the Alliance Française). Still in a remarkable state of preservation, the carving portrays a billiard table, with monkeys holding their cues as they play the game. One wonders: was this an amusing, but perceptive comment by the O'Shea brothers and their companion stone carvers – honest, hardworking and skilled craftsmen – on the rich and leisured denizens of the club?

THAT CURIOUS JAPANESE DUBLINER, LAFCADIO HEARN

1853

Lafcadio Hearn is revered in Japan as the person who wrote down everything – especially ghost stories – about the old Japan that was vanishing after 1854, when the country was opened up to the outside world. The strangest thing is that he spent his youth in Dublin.

He was born in 1850 on the Ionian island of Lefkada in a state – the Septinsular Republic – that ceased to exist in 1864: it is now part of Greece. His mother was Greek and his father an Anglo-Irish military surgeon from Dublin. Lafcadio arrived in Dublin in 1853. Abandoned at the age of four by his parents, he was brought up in Dublin by relatives. These were swindled out of their wealth when he was in his late teens. Under the name of Lafcadio Hearn he left Dublin – where he had been called 'Paddy' Hearn – and settled at the age of 19 in America: New York, Cincinnati, and as a journalist in New Orleans, as well as spending time in the West Indies. He worked for various newspapers and became famous as a writer on all that was strange, grotesque and weird. The word GUBU (see page 135) could have been invented for him!

He made a life-changing discovery in New Orleans: there was a World's Fair there in 1884–85 and he became fascinated by Japanese culture through contact with the commissioner of the Japanese pavilion. *Harper's Magazine* commissioned him in 1887 to write about Martinique, where he spent two years, and in 1890 to pen a series of articles on Japan. Hearn arrived in Yokohama in 1890 and wrote for the English-language press in Japan, and also for a number of US newspapers.

Lafcadio Hearn immediately took to Japan and its distinctive culture. Within a few months of his arrival there, he met Koizumi

Setsu, the daughter of a former samurai, and soon married her in what was one of the strangest marriages: Hearn spoke no Japanese and Setsu had little English. They had four children. He later took Japanese citizenship and changed his name to Koizumi Yakumo, meaning 'small fountain, eight clouds'.

Hearn started to write his longer works on Japanese culture: he was interested in the traditional ghost stories of Japan. He settled successively in Kobe, Matsue, then Tokyo, where he was appointed Professor, an extremely prestigious post. He died aged only 54, in Tokyo in 1904, and was cremated and buried, according to his wishes, with Buddhist rites – the first Westerner to wish to be so treated after his death.

Lafcadio Hearn was extremely famous in his lifetime. His articles in journals, and his many books about Japan, were widely admired and read. He can truly be said to be the first Westerner to get to the very soul of what it is to be Japanese. The remarkable fact is that when Japanese people today want to read about Old Japan, they have no option but to read the works of Lafcadio Hearn. Many believe him to be a native of their country, because of his adopted name. In lots of ways he is more Japanese than the Japanese themselves. Hearn's works lend themselves to film, and some of the creepiest ghost stories are adaptations. His writings from Japan are among the most important interpretations of the inner life of Japan in the English language.

One word of caution: practically every place Lafcadio Hearn lived in has been badly affected by natural disasters. His birthplace in Lefkada, a beautiful island south of Corfu, was destroyed by earthquake in 1953. Martinique was obliterated by a volcanic eruption in 1902; Kobe was destroyed by earthquake as recently as 1995; most of Tokyo was wiped out by earthquake in 1923, rebuilt, and then destroyed again, by firebombs, in 1945. The old New Orleans he knew so well succumbed to Hurricane Katrina in 2005. Only the Dublin suburbs of his boyhood remain much as he knew them ... so far!

TALES FROM THE FIELD OF DREAMS: THE CURRAGH WRENS AND BERTIE'S DISGRACE

1855

The Curragh army encampment in County Kildare, just to the West of Dublin, has been a key strategic point over recent centuries. Its central location allowed a rapid deployment of troops to secure the capital in times of strife. The setting is ideal, with wide green swards and underlying limestone. Nutritious grass and flat plains have made it particularly suitable for horses: there are many stud farms, as well as the prestigious Curragh racecourse.

It has always been a muster point for large gatherings of military forces, including during Napoleonic times. The first permanent buildings were erected here in 1855 as part of preparations for the Crimean War and it is currently the major training centre for the Irish Defence Forces.

So, back in the mid-19th century there was a big concentration of soldiers (presumably of the young and lusty variety) living in this large group of buildings, set in the middle of the great Curragh plain. The law of supply and demand prevailed and many enterprising ladies set up on the perimeter of the camp. They built what were called nests or rudimentary shacks with walls of peat, set among the clumps of furze bushes. There were ten nests in total. And there came to pass a great amount of nocturnal rustling among the furze. The ladies (young and some not so young) who inhabited this surreal world were dubbed the 'Curragh Wrens'. Life among the Wrens was surprisingly democratic – they shared the takings. However, it was not an easy life. While the soldiers could avail themselves of medical care, the women had none and venereal diseases were rife.

We now step up a royal notch. In 1861, it was decided to send the 19-year-old Prince of Wales ('Bertie') for training with the Second Battalion of the Grenadier Guards at the Curragh. It was hoped that 10 weeks of military discipline would put some backbone into the dissolute youth. He commenced his duties in July and the arrangement was that the Prince would be promoted every fortnight, so that by the time of his mother's planned visit to Ireland, she could observe her son commanding a battalion. The *Illustrated London News* breathlessly reported the princely endeavours and promotions in great detail. Victoria and Albert, on their 1861 visit to Ireland, made a day trip to the Curragh on 24 August. There was a grand review and the proud parents saw their son in full command of his troops. Albert later wrote to King William I of Prussia that Bertie 'did his part at the Curragh Camp very well'.

However, storm clouds were gathering on the horizon. It transpired that certain military officers at the Curragh, colleagues of Bertie, had inveigled one Nellie Clifden into the Prince's bedroom. She has been described as an actress, but one writer has asserted that she was a member of that standing army-in-waiting outside the gates, the Curragh Wrens. Disaster struck when the event became common knowledge in all the gentlemen's clubs across the kingdom. Jokes were made about Nellie as the 'Princess of Wales'. Prince Albert was mortified and tried to spare the Queen the disgusting details. His great fear was that the lady might get pregnant and interfere with his plans to arrange a suitable marriage for Bertie to a royal princess in Europe.

Bertie's dalliance in the Curragh was to have an unexpected consequence, one that was to cast a pall on relations with his mother for the rest of her reign. The young prince was rapidly packed off to Cambridge University, under close supervision. The Prince Consort was inconsolable; he felt that he had lost faith in his son and heir. He could not sleep. Despite not feeling well, Albert set off by train on 25 November 1861, a cold and stormy day, to meet his wayward offspring in Cambridge and remonstrate with him. On his return the next day he felt wretched and complained of weakness. He continued to decline and died on 14 December. Although in reality it is thought that stomach cancer was the cause, Queen Victoria is said to have blamed Albert's death on the chill that he caught on his visit to the errant Bertie. In a letter to her eldest daughter, Victoria, she said of Bertie, 'I never can, or ever shall, look at him without a shudder'. She regarded her son with distaste for many years after Albert's death.

ARROWS, CANNIBALS AND FINE DUBLIN WHISKEY
1857

Dublin's Natural History Museum on Merrion Square is popularly known as the 'Dead Zoo'. The opening of the museum in 1857 coincided with a public lecture by the Scottish explorer David Livingstone. With little changed since it was opened, it is a perfect example of a Victorian museum. Within are mahogany glass cabinets with trays of preserved specimens (including a collection of insects gathered by Charles Darwin). The museum holds a large amount of material from outside Ireland, a legacy of those keen Irish amateurs and scientists abroad during the 19th century. The white polar bear was donated by Sir Francis Leopold McClintock, an Irish polar explorer, who was on the mission that searched for the missing Franklin Northwest Passage expedition.

It is appropriate that the expedition theme is continued in Surgeon-Major Thomas Heazle Parke's statue in front of the museum. Parke, born in 1857, was an Irish surgeon in the British Army. He participated in the great explorer H.M. Stanley's expedition (1887–89) across Central Africa to rescue Emin Pasha, Governor of Equatoria, who had become besieged and cut off after the fall of Sudan. In the course of the expedition, Parke is reputed to have been the first European to see the Ruwenzori, or Mountains of the Moon. One remarkable event from the relief mission is depicted on the green bronze plaque, below the statue. There, Parke is seen sucking poison from an arrow wound in the chest of an expedition member. Stanley, wearing his characteristic cap, is shown on the right.

Parke is the epitome of the heroic explorer cutting through uncharted jungles, using his medical skills to save his comrades. Yet, there was another expedition member, who has earned a very much murkier reputation. This was James Sligo Jameson, grandson of John Jameson, who founded the great whiskey distilling company in Smithfield, Dublin. Born in 1856, James was both rich and footloose. He travelled widely in his twenties and visited the far shores of the British Empire including Ceylon, India, Singapore and Borneo. Africa was the new frontier, so he went to South Africa in 1878. He hunted and trekked his way to the Limpopo in Matabeleland, where he befriended the great explorer Frederick Selous. In 1881 he returned from Africa with a large collection of animal heads, insects and birds.

When Stanley was recruiting for his Emin Pasha relief expedition, Jameson offered £1,000 to be taken on, an offer that was accepted. Jameson joined Stanley at Suez in 1887. After a difficult transit through the Congo, Stanley decided to leave the sick porters and surplus stores behind, at a trading post. Jameson, to his disgust, was one of the two officers detailed to command this, dubbed the 'Rear Column'. As it turned out, this command proved to be an abject failure, due to floggings, desertions, thefts and illness. Jameson fell ill and died of a fever shortly afterwards in August 1888.

And now we get to an extraordinary turn of events. A Syrian translator, a member of the expedition, made allegations in an affidavit of 1890 of happenings that were truly out of the heart of darkness. It ran that Jameson was curious about cannibalism, which was then common among the local natives. According to the translator, Jameson wished to see it enacted. It was said that he paid six handkerchiefs for a 10-year-old girl. She was tied to a tree, killed and, in a gory scene, cut to pieces. Jameson sketched the sorry episode as it occurred. He then rendered it in watercolour. His wife denied this account, saying he had not requested the killing, but when it occurred had merely recorded it. She published his posthumous diary in 1891, in an effort to clear her husband's name.

This affair illuminates the murkier side of human existence. However, there was a curious latter-day repercussion when Jameson Irish whiskey became embroiled in a controversy after what turned out to be an unfortunate marketing campaign. In a 2011 TV commercial for the brand, it told the supposed Irish legend about a 'Hawk of Achill', which had terrorised villagers for centuries.

One day, the hawk stole a village girl and nobody took any action. When the hawk stole a barrel of Irish whiskey from John Jameson, well, 'that was another matter!' – something had to be done! With a mission to retrieve the stolen barrel, Jameson tricked the hawk by hiding in an empty whiskey barrel. The hawk fell for it and brought it back to his nest. The girl was subsequently rescued and the hawk was killed and eaten by the villagers.

This saga about the hawk, the missing girl and the eating of the hawk (with Saint-Saens' 'Danse Macabre' as the background music) sparked comments on the Internet from people who picked up eerie resonances with the event in Africa some 123 years before. In a fuss that has probably been somewhat unfair to Jameson Irish whiskey, the commercial was recently compared on Twitter with the real-life tale of the heir to the Dublin whiskey fortune, the African girl and the cannibals.

CALL OF THE WILDE: SCANDALS AND THE FALL FROM GRACE

1864

In Dublin during the Victorian era, Sir William Wilde was a prominent surgeon married to a flamboyant poet, Lady Jane Francesca Wilde, known as Speranza. They had an interesting marriage: Sir William was a philanderer and his wife had a wandering eye also. Their son Oscar garnered international fame as a writer and dramatist, but, as they say, he didn't get his talents from the wind.

Sir William combined being a pioneer in eye and ear surgery with being a gifted archaeologist, antiquarian and folklorist. He wrote widely, and among his many publications was *Lough Corrib, Its Shores and Islands*. He also founded an eye and ear hospital, the first in Britain and Ireland, to teach aural surgery. Thus Sir William was a highly respected member of high Dublin society. This was reflected when, in 1863, he was appointed as Oculist-in-ordinary to Queen Victoria. He was knighted the following year.

However, just like his son, who was to fly Icarus-like to the sun, there came a sudden fall. In the same year of his knighthood, 1864, disaster struck for Sir William as Dublin was rocked by a libel case that involved the Wildes. A legal action for libel against Lady Wilde was taken by a Miss Mary Travers, daughter of a professor at Trinity College, who was also assistant keeper to Marsh's Library. Travers had previously instituted a campaign against Sir William during which she sent letters to Dublin publications hinting that he had raped her. She had indeed become a patient of the surgeon in 1854. Travers alleged that in 1862, when she was 26 years old, Sir William had given her chloroform and next raped her. She made clear that it was the conferring of a knighthood on Wilde in January

1864 that had prompted her to take action. In the course of her campaign, Miss Travers composed a pamphlet lampooning the Wildes, characterising them as Dr and Mrs Quilp.

The outraged Lady Wilde then wrote to Mary Travers' father, expressing strongly the view that his daughter was making unfounded allegations and that he should put a stop to it. Travers found the letter and then sued Lady Wilde for libel. The young lady employed a brilliant barrister, Isaac Butt, who was also a prominent nationalist politician (Butt Bridge in Dublin is named after him). Ironically, Butt himself was a well-known rake and there was the additionally bizarre twist that he had been discovered in flagrante delicto with Lady Wilde, before her marriage. Nevertheless, he proceeded to defend his client with vigour and the court soon heard tales of embracings, fondlings and reconciliations. As can be imagined, the audience (as well as Dublin society) in those buttoned-up Victorian times found the events of the trial hugely thrilling. Sir William did not help his side of the story when he declined to appear and give evidence. After five days of the trial, the jury found in Miss Travers' favour. While the Wildes had to pay over £2,000 in costs, the court obviously did not hold much worth in Travers' virtue – she was awarded a farthing in damages.

THE RIDDLE OF ERSKINE CHILDERS, PÈRE

1870

Robert Erskine Childers was born in London in 1870; both of his parents had died by the time he was 12, and he grew up in Ireland, looked after by relatives of his mother, the Bartons of Annamoe, near Glendalough, County Wicklow. Childers graduated in Classics and Law from Cambridge, and became a parliamentary draftsman in the House of Commons. He suffered from sciatica after a fall, and switched from rugby to rowing, then to sailing. His Bostonian wife, Molly, was an invalid, and sailing was the ideal way for them to enjoy life. He came to fame in 1903 with his spy novel *The Riddle of the Sands*, which has never been out of print. It alerted Britain to the possibility of an invasion from the Frisian Islands, the string of islands off the north German coast. Childers, an excellent yachtsman, knew the islands well and he gave great realism to his novel by integrating elements from his own logbook into the story.

Having changed his political allegiance, he used his yacht, the *Asgard*, to import arms from Germany for the Irish Volunteers into Howth, in north County Dublin, in July 1914. (However, he signed up for the Royal Navy when the First World War broke out.) Some of the imported rifles were used during the Easter Rising of 1916, most notably in the General Post Office, the GPO, where the Proclamation of Independence was read out. During the ensuing War of Independence against the country of his birth he was a major force in the public relations battle. At an early stage in the discussions, Childers was a secretary to the delegates who negotiated the Anglo-Irish Treaty, signed on 6 December 1921; it was a treaty he vehemently opposed. As the Civil War progressed, the anti-Treatyites began to assassinate elected representatives, and the Free State Government, first headed by Michael Collins, retaliated by enacting extremely punitive measures: anyone in possession of an illegal weapon would be executed. Childers did possess such a weapon, a small pistol: it had been given to him as a gift by Collins himself! He was duly arrested by his erstwhile comrades in arms and sentenced to death. On the morning of 24 November 1922, he faced the firing squad in Beggar's Bush Barracks, which had been evacuated by British forces only ten months previously. His last words were: 'Take a step forward, lads – it'll be easier that way.' He instructed his son, Erskine Hamilton Childers, then 17 years old, to contact each member of the firing squad afterwards, shake their hand and forgive them.

One of Childers' anti-Treaty comrades, Seán Lemass (later to be Taoiseach), whose brother was also shot during the Civil War, made a comment on his own experience (in 1920 he was involved in the early-morning Bloody Sunday shootings under the orders of Collins): 'Firing squads don't have reunions.'

THE EMPEROR SWAPS HATS
1876

Royal visits were usually a great occasion of pomp in Dublin. This was not the case when Dom Pedro II, Emperor of Brazil, made his understated visit in 1876, though. Pedro presided over that rare thing in those times, a parliamentary monarchy. In contrast to its Latin American neighbours, Brazil was stable, experiencing economic growth and emerging as the regional power. Pedro was an erudite man, with a wide range of interests in culture and science, including astronomy. He possessed a large and wide-ranging collection of books and travelled widely in Europe and elsewhere to see the wonders of the 19th century, an enthralling period of new inventions and progress.

The monarch arrived in Dublin late one Saturday evening on a special train from Belfast. His was not the regal style and he dressed plainly. With a commanding and brisk manner, he was more interested in seeing as many of the principal sights as rapidly as possible, rather than endure the usual pomp of welcoming ceremonies. He immediately set off to inspect the great Guinness brewery at St James' Gate, which was on its way to being the largest in the world. Then it was off to catch a performance at the Gaiety Theatre.

However, the day was not over and Dom Pedro's extraordinary knowledge on the boundaries of science was to be displayed, much to the embarrassment of Dublin's first citizen. On arriving back at the Shelbourne Hotel, Pedro, despite the lateness of the hour, sent for the Lord Mayor. The worthy Mayor showed up and proceeded to talk about the great welcome to the city that awaited the Emperor. His effusive speech was cut short as Pedro announced that his sole purpose in visiting the city was to see the great telescope that the world-famous instrument-maker was currently constructing in

Dublin for Vienna. He added, 'I cannot remember the name of this great man of science, but, of course, you know whom I mean.' This drew blank looks. The Lord Mayor was nonplussed – he really had no idea to whom Dom Pedro was referring. Nevertheless, the monarch instructed the Mayor to find out and take him there the following morning.

There followed a nervous discussion between the Lord Mayor and his secretary back in the mayoral residence, the Mansion House. Eventually they remembered that there was an Astronomer Royal in the observatory in Dunsink. At eight o'clock the next morning, the Mayor's coach and pair raced up the avenue in Dunsink, transporting the anxious secretary. The Astronomer Royal, roused out of bed, confirmed that yes, such a telescope was being manufactured at the Grubb Optical and Mechanical Works in Rathmines (see pages 99–100 and 118–119), but that it was Sunday and the place would be closed. In due course, the Astronomer Royal was conveyed to breakfast with the Lord Mayor as a messenger was sent to Mr Grubb requesting that the works be opened for the visitation. The party, including the Emperor, duly arrived at Grubb's, where the telescope-maker was in attendance.

Dom Pedro turned out to be fully au fait with the intricacies of the great 27-inch telescope, currently being manufactured for the Imperial Observatory in Vienna. After a stimulating conversation, the Emperor took his leave. As he departed, he took from the hat stand what he thought was his hat. It turned out that it was Mr Grubb's new (and rather expensive) hat. Left behind was one that might have graced a cabman. It was only by chance that the Mayor's secretary noticed the error and hurriedly made the exchange for the correct apparel, just as the Emperor's carriage was about to depart.

OF TOWERS, WILD SWANS
AND HOME COMFORTS FOR
THE TROOPS
1878

Oliver St John Gogarty was the ultimate Dublin boulevardier. He was a wit, raconteur, poet and, in his day job, a surgeon. Born in 1878, he was a scion of an affluent Catholic family. Having failed his medical examinations in the Royal University (now University College Dublin) in 1898, he switched to study medicine at Trinity College. He mixed in literary circles and soon became an acquaintance of poets, including W.B. Yeats.

In 1904 Gogarty rented a Martello tower (a circular fortification built in Napoleonic times) in Sandycove to the south of Dublin. He intended to invite other young writers to stay there, to promote learning and Hellenism. James Joyce came to stay in the late summer. Relations between the two young men deteriorated and Joyce departed from the tower shortly afterwards. The tower is immortalised in the opening sequence of the novel *Ulysses*, in which the character of 'stately plump' Buck Mulligan was based on Gogarty. Joyce's description of the arch medical student was not terribly flattering: 'The plump shadowed face and sullen oval jowl recalled a prelate, patron of arts in the Middle Ages.'

Gogarty graduated in 1908, and after a sojourn in training in Vienna soon built a lucrative career as an ear, nose and throat specialist. He took the pro-Treaty side during the Irish Civil War and was nominated as a Senator in the Free State Senate. Late in 1922 the Civil War took a bitter turn with executions by the Free State of anti-Treaty fighters in tandem with reprisals by the anti-Treaty side against prominent supporters of the government, including several Members of Parliament. In January 1923 Gogarty was kidnapped by an anti-Treaty group. Brought to a house by the banks of the Liffey at Islandbridge to the west of Dublin, he managed to escape by diving into the river. Gogarty later released two swans into the river, in a ceremony attended by the then head of government, W.T. Cosgrove, and the poet W.B. Yeats, and also published a collection of poems, *An Offering of Swans*, in gratitude for his escape.

The young Gogarty was known as a prankster as well as a talented poet. When an Irish Regiment serving in the British Army returned from the Boer War in June 1900, there was a paroxysm of welcome and adulation. Gogarty duly wrote a fulsome and jingoistic 'Ode of Welcome' and sent it anonymously to the establishment and Anglo-Irish social magazine, *Irish Society*. It was published in full. The verses ran:

> The Gallant Irish yeoman
> Home from the war has come
> Each victory gained o'er foeman
> Why should our bards be dumb?
> How shall we sing their praises
> Our glory in their deeds,
> Renowned their worth amazes,
> Empire their prowess needs.
> So to Old Ireland's hearts and homes
> We welcome now our own brave boys
> In cot and Hall; 'neath lordly domes
> Love's heroes share once more our joys.
> Love is the Lord of all just now,
> Be he the husband, lover, son,
> Each dauntless soul recalls the vow
> By which not fame, but love was won.
> United now in fond embrace
> Salute with joy each well-loved face
> Yeoman: in women's hearts you hold the place.

Was Gogarty a fawning Empire loyalist? The reality turned out to be rather unexpected. It took a while for the readership to realise that the poem was an acrostic (a series of lines where the first, or other particular letters, when taken in sequence spell out a word or a phrase). In this case, discerning readers were able to put together the first letters of the poem, which gave an indelicate assessment of the impact of the regiment's return. Dublin laughed for months.

PULLING THE JOYCESTRINGS!

1882

James Joyce graduated from University College Dublin with a (very poor) Bachelor of Arts degree in 1902. Nowadays, however, this fact is overlooked. While formerly his was an unmentionable name in polite circles in Dublin, the libraries both in University College Dublin and Clongowes Wood College, where he first studied, are now named after him. We are lucky to have a few recordings of his voice, reading some of *Finnegans Wake* in his wonderful Dublin brogue, but since Bloomsweek (mid-June) 2012 we also have the opportunity to hear something that he held close to his heart (or perhaps, being Joyce, his omphalos): his very own guitar.

Dr Fran O'Rourke, a professor of philosophy at UCD, who also likes to sing Joycean songs, orchestrated the restoration of the guitar by the English luthier Gary Southwell, using the facilities of the conservation department of the National Museum of Ireland at Collins Barracks. The guitar was donated to the Joyce Tower Museum in 1966 by Joyce's friend Paul Ruggiero. The museum is in Sandycove, six miles southeast of Dublin, beside the so-called 'Forty foot' bathing-place, which used to sport the sign: 'Forty Foot Gentlemen Only'. The guitar had been on display there, silently, for 45 years. Joyce lived in the tower for less than a week, but he resurrected it for the famous opening scene in *Ulysses*.

For one week in June 2012, in celebration of the restoration of the guitar (and to recoup the cost of restoring it) as well as the passing out of copyright of the bulk of Joyce's work, lunchtime recitals were given by John Feeley, Ireland's foremost classical guitarist, and Fran O'Rourke. John Feeley is Professor of Guitar at the Dublin Institute of Technology. The recitals consisted of Irish songs from the works of James Joyce, and were held in the – very atmospheric – Physics Theatre in Newman House, on St Stephen's Green South, where Joyce attended lectures (occasionally).

The guitar, which we know was owned and played by Joyce, dates from about 1830. Mostly people have come across it in a famous photograph taken in 1915 by Joyce's friend Ottacaro Weiss in Zurich. Joyce gave the instrument to his friend Paul Ruggiero in the late 1930s, and in turn Ruggiero donated it to the Joyce Museum. The guitar, not the work of any great maker, was a fairly standard instrument of its time. It still shows signs of wear and tear made by Joyce, and left there by the restorer.

Born in Dublin in 1882, James Joyce left Ireland for Trieste in 1904, but ended up briefly in Pola in the Austro-Hungarian Empire (now Pula in Croatia). He lived with Nora Barnacle and their two children in Trieste; then in Paris, where *Ulysses* was published in 1922; and finally in Zurich, where he died in 1941, aged 59, and is buried. While the walls of the Martello tower housing the museum are made of granite eight feet thick to withstand the rigours of a possible French invasion, anyone who reads Joyce's very private love letters to Nora sent from Dublin while on a brief visit in 1909 requires fairly thick skin: they are not so much logical or eschatological, but plain scatological. As they say in Dublin: 'You could sing that!'

DECLARATION OF LIQUID
INDEPENDENCE
1888

Dublin's suburbs grew and grew during the Victorian era. The largest of these was Rathmines, located just to the south of the Grand Canal. The dynamic for this was the unusual mix of politics and religion that simmered in the city at that time. When the last legal restrictions on Catholics were removed in 1829 there was a power shift away from the Protestant Ascendancy. Catholics began to be elected to Dublin Corporation. Many were of the aspirant class of grocers and vintners. The Corporation also began to take on a nationalist hue. This was unpalatable to the well-off. As the central city began to get run-down and some elegant Georgian squares were on their way to becoming slum tenements, there was a flight of the middle class from the centre.

Rathmines was there to welcome them! The township was controlled by property developers and their cohorts. Fine new squares, villas and terraced streets were constructed. Expenditure on items such as roads was kept to a minimum, with the intention of keeping rates (a tax on property) low. This resulted in the roads of the township being dusty in the summer and muddy in winter. Special crossing points were put in to allow ladies, in their long skirts, to cross roads with decorum and without collecting too much mud in the process. So, life was very pleasant for the affluent in this leafy suburb.

Trouble was looming, however. Water supply in the 19th century had been ad hoc and unreliable. As medical science advanced, there was a realisation that clean water and proper drainage were necessary to keep diseases like cholera and typhoid at bay. Dublin Corporation came up with an ambitious scheme to capture the abundant waters of the rivers that flowed from the mountains to the South of the city and pipe them back to Dublin. They had the temerity to make an offer to householders in Rathmines that they would extend water pipes to each house and provide potable water. The horrified township refused this physical manifestation of the tentacles of the enemy. Meanwhile, Rathmines persisted in extracting water as it had done for decades, taking it from the Grand Canal. Residents continued to endure the foreign bodies and strange creatures that they found in their water. Some wrote outraged letters to the newspapers. Eventually the township decided to build a new dedicated reservoir in a valley to the West of Dublin, and by 1888 pure Rathmines water flowed, unsullied by any connection to that of Big Brother across the canal.

Dublin Corporation had also sensibly suggested collaboration in the expensive business of constructing a new and comprehensive drainage system in the city. Again, this was to no avail. The peculiar mix of paranoia and aversion to the perceived grasping embrace of Dublin Corporation led to this incongruous roar of the municipal mouse: 'Rathmines will drain alone,' thundered across the Rathmines township council chamber. Eventually Rathmines and its equally affluent neighbour, Pembroke Township, constructed their own system. Thus, by the late 1870s, their combined aristocratic effluent flowed along by the Grand Canal and was deposited in Dublin Bay.

THE RAJ IN NORTH DUBLIN: THE SURPRISING ECLECTICISM OF McKEE BARRACKS

1889

Travel to the west of Dublin, along the north bank of the Liffey. Just past Heuston Station, you soon come to the main entrance gate to that great lung of Dublin, the Phoenix Park. Here you can enjoy the trees, the deer and the green expanses. Look to the eastern side of the park and you can just about see, above a long boundary wall, a series of buildings in bright red brick, with tips of the protruding green copper turrets just in sight. This is an army barracks, originally Marlborough Cavalry Barracks, now called McKee (after a republican leader who was shot in 1920 while in custody of the British during the War of Independence). Currently it houses an infantry battalion and an artillery regiment of the Irish Army. It is also the headquarters of the Army Equitation School, whose impeccably groomed horses can be seen in competition at various venues including the annual Dublin Horse Show.

In most countries, buildings in army barracks are utilitarian, with plain frontages and little decoration. This is radically different in the case of McKee Barracks. Built in the late Victorian era, with work beginning in 1889, this is an outpouring of exuberance. It has an eclectic mix of turrets, great chimney stacks and a multitude of dormer windows, which all blend together successfully. The different types of building within the barracks are all unified by this vigorous red-brick theme. The overwhelming combination of pinnacled red brick and cupolas gives echoes of Imperial adventures and the Raj.

Tales abound about this eclectic barracks. People, used to the plainer type of barracks all over Ireland, speculate that it was all down to a mistake. It is said there was an error made when the plans were dispatched from the Royal Engineers in England. The story runs that these plans were inadvertently switched with those for a similar barracks to be built in British India, then at the height of its splendour. Sadly, there is no evidence for this. Even though many Irish troops served in British India, there is no sign anywhere on the subcontinent of any great forbidding army barracks of granite or limestone built in the severe Irish style. Probably the most surprising part of this story is that McKee Barracks was the product of the architectural department of the Royal Engineers, a sober and regimented body not known for its wild eclecticism.

AS REGARDS ASGARDS
1904

The original yacht, the *Asgard*, the most famous ship in recent Irish history, was built in 1904 by Colin Archer, a Norwegian boat-builder of Scottish ancestry. He had also built the *Fram*, from whence Roald Amundsen made his first expedition to the South Pole. When Robert Erskine Childers (see pages 90-1) married Molly Osgood, her wealthy father gave them *Asgard* as a wedding present. The vessel, 51 feet long and weighing 22 tons, was purchased in Norway for £1,000, an enormous sum at the time.

The yacht played a pivotal role in the pre-Rising 1914 gun-running operation, masterminded by Erskine Childers, when it landed its load of (antiquated Prussian War) rifles and ammunition for the Irish Volunteers at Howth harbour, near Dublin, where the event is commemorated by a plaque.

While the first *Asgard* was being stored in Kilmainham Gaol, another vessel, the *Asgard II*, was built in Arklow, Co. Wicklow, and launched in 1981 as the Irish national sail-training vessel. The beautifully masted shape of *Asgard II* graced the oceans and seas until one night in September 2008, when it apparently hit a submerged object in the Bay of Biscay and sank rapidly, fortunately without loss of life. Resting 90 yards deep, 25 miles from the coast of France, she was not salvaged.

In 2012 Nessa Childers MEP, granddaughter of the original owners, was guest of honour when the restored yacht was 'launched' at the opening of a new permanent exhibition, '*Asgard*: The 1914 Howth Gun-Running Vessel Conserved', at the National Museum of Ireland, Collins Barracks. The only ship previously exhibited there was a Viking vessel, the *Sea Stallion*, which was a replica of a ship built of Wicklow oak in around 1042. The *Sea Stallion* from Glendalough, to give her full name, arrived at Malahide Marina on

11 August 2007 and was taken to the huge courtyard in the National Museum, where it remained on show to the people of Dublin. The 30m-long warship was a replica of a vessel named *Skuldelev 2*, which was built in Dublin by Vikings using Scandinavian ship-building methods. Since it had a crew of about 70 warriors, it was probably the ship of an important Viking chieftain, and one of those ocean-going longships that the Viking sagas mention.

DINNEEN'S WONDERFUL
ONE-MAN DICTIONARY
1904

Dublin's strangest lexicographical tale is that of Father Patrick S. Dinneen. The dictionary he produced is in use to this day and is known simply as *Dinneen*, famous for its exuberance, the humour of its definitions and the nuttiness of its flavour, as well as of its author. Supposedly a dictionary of modern Irish, it is in fact one of the world's great dictionaries for browsing – like an encyclopaedia of medieval, pre-industrial manners, customs, lore, skills and crafts – it has been digitised and is now available online. Truly, Dinneen made modern Irish a language out of what J.P. Mahaffy has described as a patois. Dinneen, working for many long years at his desk in the National Library of Ireland, wrote himself into the list of Irish people who will always be remembered. The dictionary is printed in the older Gaelic font, and if ever there was an incentive for learning to read those few letters that show any major differences, being able to read Dinneen is it.

Born in 1860 in Sliabh Luachra, County Kerry, on the borders with County Cork, Father Patrick spent the years from 1880 to 1900 as a Jesuit priest. He then resigned, never to practise again as a priest. At first he lived in a caravan in Malahide, County Dublin, with good access by train to the National Library of Ireland in Kildare Street. He devoted himself to the Irish language with a passion and, rather than merely talking about it, he wrote a great number of books in record time. But the book by which he will be best remembered, his monument, is the volume entitled *Irish Texts Society: Foclóir Gaedhilge agus Béarla*. An Irish-English dictionary being a thesaurus of the words, phrases and idioms of the modern Irish language, with explanations in English, compiled and edited

Dublin's Strangest Tales

by Rev. Patrick S. Dinneen, MA Dublin, first published in 1904.

Containing about 30,000 headwords in Irish, it was a remarkable feat completed in just three years. Whereas nowadays dictionaries are compiled using a corpus of material in digital form, in his time there were few books in print, or even printed books, in Irish. His task was all the more difficult because most material in Irish was preserved in manuscript form by families of hereditary keepers. Although there had been Irish-English dictionaries before this, his volume brought the Irish language, an ancient Celtic tongue, into a new era. He was conscious of the delicate nature of his task: on the one hand he wished to record those words that were in the literature, and which could be used in modern life. But he also knew that recording those words in use in the scattered areas where it was still spoken as the vernacular was vital if the language was to survive.

Dinneen's dictionary in its first edition was not a large book; it suffered the ignominious fate of having its stock and plates destroyed in the fires in O'Connell Street in the 1916 Rising. With hindsight this was a lucky stroke: Dinneen, with characteristic zeal, set about a second edition, which is more than twice as large. The 1927 'greatly enlarged' edition consists of some 1,300 double-columned pages of closely printed text. This edition became a classic, and has never gone out of print. It was used – of necessity – by all who wanted to understand Irish until 1979, when a totally new dictionary in roman type was published. However, Dinneen's work was in many ways irreplaceable: his style was inimitable, and full of the peculiar wit practised in his own life. Most serious readers of Irish use both the modern dictionary and *Dinneen*. There are many classic definitions which are now known as 'Dinneenisms'.

His desk in the National Library of Ireland, where he worked on the first edition from 1901 until 1903, now bears a commemorative plaque. However, Dinneen was not without his blemishes. He engaged in a ferocious fight with another language enthusiast, Michael O'Hickey (Micheál Ó hÍcí), with drops of academic venom being spilled liberally in every direction. The lore of *Dinneen* has been revitalised in recent years by Biddy Jenkinson, who has transformed him into a demon detective in the Sherlock Holmes' tradition. Guess who wins when the rival detectives compete?

One of the duties of boy attendants was to follow Dinneen as he left the reading room, picking up the slips of paper that fell from him 'like leaves from autumn trees', on which were written the entries for the forthcoming dictionary. For the second edition he used the National Museum, on the other side of Leinster House: the seat of Dáil Éireann, the Irish Parliament.

The following examples give a flavour of the contents of this most eccentric dictionary:

> *bleachtaire*: a milker, a dairyman, a milk-dealer; a wheeler; a detective.
>
> *buarach bháis*: an unbroken hoop of skin cut with incantations from a corpse across the entire body from shoulder to footsole and wrapped in silk of the colours of the rainbow and used as a spancel to tie the legs of a person to produce certain effects of witchcraft.
>
> *fóidín mearaidhe*: a little sod on which if one tread he is led away and has to keep walking aimlessly till moonrise unless he turn his coat inside out.
>
> *maide fóir*: a stick swathed around with a straw rope used by hens as a gangway to reach the roost.
>
> *maothachán*: an emollient liquid for steeping, esp. suds and urine stored for washing new flannel, tucking frieze, etc. (the consumption of cabbage affected its emollient qualities).
>
> *tiachóg*: a bag made of sheepskin, a bag for hens to lay eggs in, a wallet for miscellaneous use according to the season of the year.

Those using the National Library remember him as a gentle, shabby old man chewing apples and raw carrots with a pile of books around him like a rampart. In 1934 he collapsed on the steps of the National Library and was taken to hospital, protesting, 'Take me home, hospitals are too expensive.' He died within a few days and was given a state funeral at Glasnevin Cemetery, on Dublin's northside.

THE RIDDLE OF ERSKINE CHILDERS, FILS

1905

After his father's execution, Childers fils, also born in London, in 1905, went on to become a minister in 1951 in a government headed by Eamon de Valera. It is quite strange that he became the first citizen of Ireland, since neither he nor either of his parents was born in Ireland: he had become a naturalised Irish citizen in 1938, under a provision of the Irish Nationality and Citizenship Act of 1935 that allowed for citizenship in special cases: 'The Executive Council may, if and whenever they so think proper, cause a certificate of naturalisation to be issued under this Act to any person or to a child or grandchild of any person who, in the opinion of the Executive Council, has done signal honour or rendered distinguished service to the Irish Nation.' Childers père and de Valera had been among the most visceral opponents of the Treaty of 1921, and it looks as if this section could have been drafted with Childers fils in mind.

When President John F. Kennedy came on his famous State visit to Ireland in June 1963, he was greeted by President de Valera, and also by Childers, who was Minister for Transport and Power. Five months later de Valera attended Kennedy's funeral. Erskine Hamilton Childers went on to be elected fourth President of Ireland, immediately after de Valera's two terms as President had ended, in 1973. Childers was the only President to die in office, in 1974. De Valera outlived him by a year.

The family's interest in politics has continued to a further generation: the President's daughter, Nessa Childers, is a Member of the European Parliament for the Irish Labour Party.

FROM SILK KIMONOS TO THE BARRICADES: THE STORMY CAREER OF COUNTESS MARKIEWICZ

1905

There is an intriguing painting, now in the possession of a private collector in Dublin, entitled 'The Investiture of the Earl of Mayo as Knight of St Patrick 1905'. The painting of this event in St Patrick's Hall in Dublin Castle, by Prince Casimir Dunin Markiewicz, was described at the time as amateurish, but within there is rich social detail. The Knights of St Patrick, in a similar manner to the Knights of the Garter, was an arrangement that allowed the Hibernian haute-bourgeoisie to dress up in majestic medieval regalia and assemble on grand occasions. This 'chivalrous order' had been founded by King George III in 1783 and, with the Sovereign as head of the order, it proved to be one of the vehicles to tie the Anglo-Irish establishment to the British crown.

Among the cast of characters in the 1905 painting, standing to the right of the vice-regal dais, pride of place goes to Lord Mayo. He and his wife were important figures in the cultural world of Ireland in the early 20th century. Ranged around are the Prince of Wales (later to become King George V), the Viceroy, plus various officers of the British army and navy. There is a page, a mace bearer, and the Ulster King of Arms. In addition to pillars of the establishment, there is a host of Irish lords, from Lord Bandon to Lord Waterford. Lord Lucan is there – obviously unaware of what his descendant was to get up to – decades later. There are some ladies in the audience. Who is the demure young woman in a green dress, quietly looking on? It is none other than Constance, Countess Markiewicz, wife of the artist.

So far, so bourgeois. However, the surprising thing is the later career of the young lady, who quickly metamorphosed from the eminently respectable world of Dublin Castle society into being one of the most fervent revolutionaries of Nationalist Ireland. Constance Gore-Booth came from a landowning family with large estates in County Sligo. They lived at Lissadell House, where the poet W.B. Yeats was a constant visitor. Later he famously described Constance and her sister Eva in a poem as:

> The light of evening, Lissadell,
> Great windows open to the south,
> Two girls in silk kimonos, both
> Beautiful, one a gazelle.

Constance met Casimir when both were art students at the Académie Julian in Paris. They married and returned to Dublin, settling for a while in Frankfort Avenue, in Rathgar. Casimir was a theatrical set designer and the couple took part in amateur dramatic productions. In those days Rathgar was eminently middle class. Perhaps Constance was showing her rebellious streak early, but the story runs that when she was seen doing gardening and wheeling a wheelbarrow down Frankfort Avenue, the neighbourhood was scandalised.

In the years that followed, the couple separated and Casimir returned to Poland. Now Constance's career moved up several notches, from the sedate to the astonishing. She joined Sinn Féin in 1908 and quickly became immersed in the struggle for Irish independence. When the Rising broke out in Dublin in Easter 1916, Constance, Countess Markiewicz, was manning the barricades, gun in hand. She was second in command of the (socialist) Citizen Army, which took over the Royal College of Surgeons at the western end of St Stephen's Green. After several days of fierce fighting the outnumbered rebels surrendered. The Countess was put in solitary confinement in Kilmainham Gaol. The leaders of the rising were soon court-martialled. Sixteen were shot.

Constance was tried, with one of the charges being that she 'did an act to wit did take part in an armed rebellion against His Majesty the King'. The irony of it was that 11 years before, she had been the modest young lady seated in St Patrick's Hall, only a few yards away from the man who was now the reigning King, George V. Constance was found guilty and sentenced to death by firing squad. The sentence was confirmed but was commuted to penal servitude for life, on grounds of her sex.

Along with other rebels, Constance was released under an amnesty in 1917. She continued her revolutionary career and was elected as a Sinn Féin Member of Parliament, the first woman to be elected to the Westminster Parliament. In line with Sinn Féin policy, she did not take up her seat. When Sinn Féin set up its own Parliament in Dublin, she was appointed Minister for Labour in 1919, thus becoming the first woman to be appointed a Cabinet Minister in Europe. Constance had a dusty view of the idea of a woman dominating by 'careful manipulation of her sex and her good looks'. Instead she suggested that the ideal for women in the everyday world would be to 'dress suitably in short skirts and strong boots, leave your jewels and gold wands in the bank and buy a revolver. Don't trust to your "feminine charm" and your capacity for getting on the soft side of men, but take up your responsibilities and be prepared to go your own way.'

She was arrested many times, on one occasion for what was regarded as a seditious speech, where she repeated Jonathan Swift's dictum of two centuries before: 'burn everything British but its coal'. As the War of Independence developed she went on the run. Still working as a minister, she had a ladder set outside her office in case there was a police raid.

In 1921 there was a truce with Britain. Constance was opposed to the subsequent Treaty and took the anti-Treaty side in the Civil War that raged in 1922–23. After the war she was elected as a member of the Dáil (parliament) for the new Fianna Fáil party. When she died in 1927 she was given a public funeral and was buried in the Republican Plot in Glasnevin Cemetery in Dublin. Eamon de Valera (a fellow 1916 leader whose sentence of death had also been commuted, and who later became President of Ireland) gave the funeral oration for this extraordinary debutante – turned fiery – revolutionary.

HITLER AND THE HORSESHOE BAR
1910

The Shelbourne Hotel is an iconic structure in Dublin. Its red-brick bulk presents a slightly clunky frontage that can be seen from the leafy square of St Stephen's Green. It has been significantly modernised in recent years and is now operated by an international chain, but it still manages to exude the feel of the best of a Victorian hotel. The wrought-iron facade, the high and elegant ceilings with elaborate covings and plasterwork, maintain the 19th-century air of graciousness in this, the premier hotel of the city.

It has long been a haunt of the rich and aristocratic. Many deals, political and business, have been made in the Horseshoe Bar. The Irish Constitution was drafted in a room here, now known as the Constitution Room.

One Martin Burke from Tipperary created the hotel in 1824 by acquiring and adapting three of the townhouses on the northern end of St Stephen's Green. It was radically rebuilt in the 1860s under the direction of architect John McCurdy. He was fresh from his design of the large extension of Kilmainham Gaol on the outskirts of Dublin, having created the airy and spacious east wing there, which employed the new and progressive techniques in the design of Victorian penal institutes. One wonders why McCurdy was selected but, on reflection, there is not much difference in the design task between a hotel and a prison, each comprising a successive series of rooms along a corridor. (The gaol cells would possibly be a trifle more Spartan!) In front of the grand and imposing entrance can be seen the dramatic figures of Nubian princesses and their slave girls, all holding a lamp on high. The two statues of slave girls can be distinguished by the shackles on their legs. These bronze statues were cast in the Paris studio of a Monsieur Barbazet. Local wits at the time claimed that these were the only four virgins left in Dublin.

The Shelbourne has a surprising association with a dark figure from the 20th century. Adolf Hitler's half-brother, Alois Jnr, worked there as a waiter in the early 1900s. Born in 1882, Alois was the son of Alois Hitler Snr. On the death of his wife, Alois Snr remarried and in 1889, a new cuddly baby boy arrived, who was named Adolf. Life in the Hitler household was fraught and Alois Jnr soon left. Something of a drifter, he arrived in Dublin and secured a position as a waiter in the Shelbourne Hotel. In due course he met a local girl, Bridget Dowling, at the Dublin Horse Show in 1909.

Alois cut a dash and claimed that he was a German hotelier on tour. After assiduous courting, Bridget consented to marry the dashing Austrian and they moved to Liverpool in 1910. Their son, Michael Patrick Hitler, was born a year later. Alois Jnr did not prove to be too uxorious and left in 1914 for a gambling tour. Cut off by the war, he never returned from Germany. He abandoned his family and began a new career selling safety-razors. He had word passed to his wife that he was dead and then remarried bigamously. After many vicissitudes, Bridget and her son eventually settled in the United States.

RED VANS:
SOAP AND SWASTIKAS
1912

Imagine you are visiting Dublin in the 1970s, and partaking of refreshment in a city hostelry. As you relax there you might look out to the street, through a pane darkly. Prepare yourself for the bizarre. Indeed, you might well splutter into your pint as you see an astonishing sight. There, prominently emblazoned on a passing van, is a Swastika. *Gott im Himmel*, what is going on? Did the Nazis escape to Dublin and hole up here, instead of some steamy forest in Argentina or Paraguay? Is it the 'Boys from Dublin', rather than from Brazil?

Relax; take another sip of your pint. The origins of all this were of a peaceful nature, more associated with soapsuds than savagery. In 1912, in the Dublin suburb of Ballsbridge, a laundry was founded which chose the (then innocuous) swastika as its symbol. Over the following decades the company's electric vans were a common sight in Dublin. They glided quietly around the city, painted in red with a black swastika set against a white background, making deliveries and collecting laundry. The laundry premises itself was surmounted by a large chimney, which towered over the surrounding area. The large swastika set at the top of the chimney could be seen from afar.

Swastika comes from the Sanskrit svastika, meaning 'favourable to wellbeing'. Over the ages it has been a symbol of prosperity and good luck. Rudyard Kipling used it as an insignia in his books. In Norse mythology, the hammer-wielding god Thor is associated with storms and healing. The swastika was the sign for Thor's hammer in Scandinavia and it had been used as a symbol by the Finnish Air force. However, the unfortunate emblem's brush with notoriety came when the swastika was adopted by the National Socialist

Party, founded in Germany in 1919. It was incorporated into the national German flag in September 1935. As they say, the rest is history, and the emblem became indelibly associated with tyranny, brutality and the bloody Second World War.

Meanwhile, back in Dublin, the extraordinary thing was that the laundry held its nerve. They did not budge and continued to use their chosen symbol, the swastika. They had selected this symbol of wellbeing in 1912, and saw no reason to change, even if some latter-day parvenus on the Continent had subsequently chosen to use it. In 1939, to make it clear that it was there first, the laundry changed its name to the 'Swastika Laundry (1912)'. The Swastika business was eventually taken over by another laundry company in the late 1960s but the swastika logo continued in use well into the 1980s.

A SLICE OF TORTURED BACON
1915

The Dublin City Gallery on Parnell Square (also known as the Hugh Lane) is a wonderful place to visit. Large and grand, it was formerly the town house of the Earl of Charlemont. One of the finer buildings of Georgian Dublin, it was designed by Sir William Chambers, remembered also for his design of Somerset House in London. The restored building is now home to exceptional Irish and continental paintings. At the core of the collection are the outstanding Impressionist paintings left by bequest of Sir Hugh Lane. Sir Hugh, an Irishman who had made his fortune in the London art world, was drowned when the liner *Lusitania* was torpedoed in 1915, ironically just off his native county, Cork.

As in most galleries there is a serene air throughout. However, at one end, you have to brace yourself and prepare for the unexpected. Newly installed here is the reconstructed studio of the artist Francis Bacon, now posthumously garnering even more fame than during his lifetime. His work is certainly fashionable – Bacon's painting of a male nude sold in 2012 for the breathtaking sum of $44m.

Bacon was born in Baggot Street in Dublin in 1909. After experiencing Paris and decadent Weimar Berlin in his early years he eventually moved to London, where he spent the rest of his life. A bon vivant he passed his time drinking, gambling and hanging out with the louche Soho set. Despite this he churned out great paintings with an existential edge, including his Study after Velázquez's 'Portrait of Pope Innocent X'. One might say that perhaps a good dose of decadence can help make you a better painter. Bacon died in 1992 and his heir donated the contents of his studio to the Hugh Lane Gallery. The studio at 7 Reece Mews in London was dismantled and relocated to Dublin, where it was painstakingly reconstructed.

Get ready to descend into chaos. You can look from well-sited vantage points around the periphery at the dissolute clutter within. Inside these original walls are slashed canvases, books, magazines and drawings. So, was this Dubliner a tortured genius? Margaret Thatcher certainly thought so. She described him as 'that man who paints those dreadful pictures'. In the Hugh Lane Gallery you can get an insight into his brilliant mind and the idiosyncratic way he produced his paintings.

RUSSIA AND THE CURIOUS TALE OF THE RATHMINES' ACCENT
1920

Dublin's suburb of Rathmines developed during the 19th century. The area has declined somewhat over recent decades and is now a mixture of comfortable houses and run-down blocks of flats, popular with students. Some parts of it could now be considered as having a left-bank atmosphere. However, 100 years ago, it was a highly desirable place to live and the accent there was perceived as 'posh'.

And so it came about that one Roderick (Roddy) Connolly visited Bolshevik Russia in 1920, where he met Vladimir Ilyich Lenin, the Russian leader. Young Roddy had an impeccable revolutionary pedigree. Although only 15 years of age, he had run messages for the rebels during the Easter Rising in 1916. His father, James, had been one of the leaders of the Rising and was executed afterwards, although wounded, strapped to a chair. In 1921 Roddy Connolly helped found the Communist Party of Ireland and became its President.

In the late 1970s, Connolly gave a lecture in Dublin, where he spoke of his visit to Petrograd (now St Petersburg). A short silent film was shown, where the youthful Connolly was seen walking, in conversation with the bearded leader of the Bolshevik government. A member of the audience later asked Connolly if he could speak Russian, as there was no interpreter present. 'No,' replied Connolly, 'Lenin could speak English, and do you know, the strange thing is that he spoke it with a Rathmines' accent!' It has been subsequently claimed that Lenin was taught English during his stay in London in 1902, by an Irishwoman who had lived in Rathmines.

This modest Dublin suburb has another, this time fortuitous, connection with revolutionary Russia. Look along the main

Rathmines Road and you'll find it is dominated by the great green copper dome of the Mary Immaculate Refuge of Sinners Catholic Church. An electrical fault caused a fire here in 1920 and the church burned down, its dome collapsing. A major reconstruction was undertaken over the following years. It was Rathmines' fortune that they secured a new dome, which had been made in Glasgow, at an advantageous price. It had been made for a Russian orthodox church in Tsarist St Petersburg and ordered prior to the Revolution in 1917. Obviously churches or their domes were not in demand under the new Bolshevik regime and the order had been cancelled. So, it transpired that Russia's loss was Dublin's (and Rathmines') gain.

AN ERRANT SHELL FALLS
ON ITS DONORS
1922

The Anglo-Irish Treaty, where the terms for British withdrawal from Ireland were set out, was ratified in January 1922. The Provisional Government (which became the Irish Free State) set up a national army and the British Army prepared to evacuate their barracks. On 15 January 1922 the evacuation got under way in Dublin Castle, over the centuries the seat of British power in Ireland. Michael Collins, the Irish leader, arrived in a taxi to participate in the handover ceremony. The British officer in charge remonstrated with Collins for being seven and a half minutes late. Collins laughed and exclaimed, 'After seven and a half centuries, you're welcome to the seven and a half minutes!'

However, jollity did not follow. There was a split between those in the new government, who reluctantly agreed to accept the terms of the Treaty, and those in the IRA, who could not stomach its provisions. Early 1922 proved to be a confused time, with minor confrontations between the opposing sides. In a decisive move, the Republican forces occupied the Four Courts, with its long imposing facade along the Liffey Quays. It is in a central and strategic location but perhaps one that a force whose main experience was of guerrilla warfare should not have holed up in. Meanwhile the British forces were still ensconced in barracks around Ireland preparing plans to withdraw. The Free State Army rapidly began to recruit and train.

In June 1922 the Assistant Chief-of-Staff of the Free State Army was kidnapped. This proved to be the last straw. The Free State forces obtained two 18-pounder field guns and shells from the British Army and after four o'clock in the morning of 28 June 1922 the guns opened up. These were positioned on streets to the south of the river, shielded by armoured Lancia trucks. Over the next two days the great grey granite walls of the Four Courts were pounded, with machine guns rattling and sniper fire flying from both sides. More field guns were obtained from the British, who looked on the fratricidal conflict with no small feelings of Schadenfreude. The guns boomed and shells flew north across the Liffey, creating gaps in the walls of what is one of Dublin's finest Georgian public buildings.

In the middle of the din came the surprising news: the British positions were under fire from what had been, a day or two before, their very own guns! It transpired that a shell had fallen on the Royal Hospital complex in Kilmainham, built at the end of the 17th century as a home for former British soldiers – the Chelsea Hospital was modelled on this. It was also the headquarters of the British Commander-in-Chief. The shell had travelled in a westerly direction from the conflict downriver. What was going on? After a hurried investigation a general of the Free State Army went to the British military headquarters to explain and apologise. Additional 18-pounder guns had been situated to the rear of the Four Courts complex, to continue the assault from the North. It transpired that a young and inexperienced gunner located there had canted his artillery gun on high. He had been aiming over open sights at a sniper on the great dome of the Four Courts. The shell went straight through the dome and sailed on up to Kilmainham.

Eventually on 30 June 1922 the defenders surrendered, but not before a massive explosion had obliterated most of the priceless collection in Ireland's Public Record Office, located in the Four Courts complex. The Civil War soon became one of guerrilla war in the Irish countryside, and ground to a bloody end by May of the following year.

BRENDAN BEHAN'S
POSTHUMOUS LIFE
IN GREECE
1923

The Dublin playwright Brendan Behan rarely minced his words. On landing in Mallorca in 1959, at the height of his fame, when he was asked, 'What would you most like to see in Spain?' he replied, 'Franco's funeral!' He was immediately deported back to Ireland.

Born in 1923, he grew up on Dublin's north side in a Republican family. His mother had been involved in the 1916 Rising and the War of Independence. The brains behind the latter was the youthful Michael Collins, who was later – during the Irish Civil War, in August 1922 – assassinated in his home county, Cork, by his former fighting colleagues. It was a terrible blow to the infant Free State, of which Collins was one of the first leaders. In 1936, at the age of 13, Behan wrote a lament for Collins called 'The Laughing Boy': the name his mother gave her friend Collins, even though they took opposing sides in the Civil War.

Behan spent several years of his life in prison because of his Republican activities. What ended up as his most famous play, *The Hostage*, started as a short one-act play in Irish (Gaelic), first performed in Dublin in 1957. Following its success, Behan made an English version, expanding into a full-length play, under the guidance of the avant-garde producer Joan Littlewood, director of the Theatre Workshop in Stratford East, London. *The Hostage* was first produced in Stratford on 14 October 1958 to great acclaim. Behan had been influenced by the German playwright Berthold Brecht: the characters in *The Hostage* frequently burst into song. In his haste to finalise the English version, he included his youthful poem, 'The Laughing Boy'.

On 20 March 1964 Brendan Behan died in Dublin of a combination of alcoholism and diabetes. Over 100,000 people attended his funeral: one of the biggest since Collins himself had been buried in the same cemetery, a year before Behan's birth. They are buried not far from each other in Glasnevin Cemetery.

Behan's *The Hostage* had a strange afterlife in Greece, a country he never visited. After a performance in English in Paris, it came to the attention of the Greek composer Míkis Theodorákis, then living in Paris. He composed the music for a cycle of songs, lyrics were translated into Greek in 1961 and it was called *Enas Omiros* ('A Hostage'). The play was successfully produced in Athens. Theodorákis' music of Behan's *The Hostage* took on yet another new life: the director Kosta-Gavras wished to make a film of the notorious assassination in Thessaloniki in 1963 of a Greek MP. The name of this gripping film is *Z* (1969). Kosta-Gavras had wanted Theodorákis to compose new music especially for it. However, Theodorákis was incommunicado in internal exile in Greece, and even his exact whereabouts were unknown. Kosta-Gavras decided instead to re-use Theodorákis' music for *Enas Omiros*, with 'The Laughing Boy' as the theme music.

In Greece it was usually assumed that the lyrics of this song, sung in Greek, referred to the assassinated politician, who had become a cult figure for Greek youth; in fact they clearly refer to Michael Collins, who was also assassinated by his own people, in tragic circumstances.

The film *Z* and its soundtrack were circulated illegally in Greece, and immediately became powerful symbols of opposition to the military dictatorship. As a rallying call for opponents of the regime it was hugely important in drawing attention to the junta's denial of human rights, and became a cult film. When the colonels were eventually ousted in 1974, there was a huge concert to express the joy of liberty. The song on everyone's lips was 'The Laughing Boy'. Hearing it sung even today is a riveting experience, as it is one of Theodorákis' best compositions.

The song still lives on, and is known by a huge number of the Greek population, even if they are hardly aware of the Irish origins of the lyrics they know so well.

Brendan Behan, no friend of dictatorships, would have been delighted to know that the poem he wrote as a teenager lived on in a film made after his death, and that both the song and the film had been banned in Greece by military decree!

MUSSOLINI'S
UNSETTLING GIFT
1933

The Italian dictator Benito Mussolini never visited Dublin. So why is there a gift from him to be found in the city, a painting that still hangs in a fine building near St Stephen's Green in the centre of Dublin? The genesis of all this is complicated. The building, Iveagh House, is now the rather opulent headquarters of the Irish Department of Foreign Affairs. This was originally built as two town houses during the Georgian era. It was acquired by Sir Benjamin Lee Guinness (grandson of the founder of the brewery, Arthur Guinness) in 1862. He combined the two houses and extensively renovated them in a magnificent and expansive style. Sir Benjamin's son, Lord Iveagh, lived there and the building was donated to the Irish state in 1939.

So, how did Mussolini's painting get there? After a career as a journalist and agitator, Mussolini became Prime Minister of Italy in 1922. He rapidly consolidated his grip on power and had some early (if perhaps superficial) successes in boosting the economy and carrying out such public works as draining the Pontine Marshes and, famously, making the Italian trains run on time. In 1929, he concluded the Lateran Treaty with the Vatican, which settled the long-running disputes over the previous loss of Papal lands and is the basis on which the mini-state functions in the heart of Rome to this very day.

This, then, was the background when Éamon de Valera, Taoiseach (prime minister) of Éire, came to visit Rome in May 1933. Mussolini, although a thoroughgoing dictator, had, as we have seen, regularised matters with the Vatican and Italy was an important power on the world stage. De Valera acted as his own foreign minister and had been President of the League of Nations. He had made a keynote speech at its session of September 1932 on the necessity for all states, large or small, to abide by the League's obligations. As it happens, it was only later in 1935 that, flouting the strictures of the League of Nations, Mussolini embarked on his brutal invasion of Ethiopia.

De Valera duly visited the Vatican, did some sightseeing of Roman antiquities and made a visit to the Italian king. He then met the dictator and no doubt there were some substantive discussions on League of Nations affairs. Mussolini gave the Irish leader a gift of a painting by Giorgio de Chirico. De Chirico was an Italian painter born in 1888, and one of the founders of the style of metaphysical painting. This is the use of disquieting symbolic figures, creating an uneasy feeling in the viewer. From the 1920s de Chirico became interested in a return to the Italian classical condition. Some of his works from that period have been seen as being in harmony with the fascist culture of heroic, almost homoerotic, comradeship promulgated under Mussolini's dictatorship. The painting in Dublin is thought to date from the 1920s. It shows two men riding horses with another sitting by a barren seashore. This unsettling painting is in the neo-classical style and the near-naked men could be from ancient Rome or Greece. With a small classical building in the background and a piece of a fluted stone column resting on the ground the allusion is emphasised.

So, through the black arts of diplomacy and affairs of state of the 1930s, this is how a fine if disquieting painting, donated by one of the 20th century's greatest dictators, came to be hanging on the wall of the ante-room to the Minister's office at Iveagh House in St Stephen's Green.

ON NEUTRAL TURF:
TALES OF BETJEMAN
1941

Dublin's suburban trains are now sleek vehicles, which travel smoothly and silently along the great sweep of Dublin Bay from Howth in the North to Bray in the South. It was not always thus: pre-1960s steam engines chuffed along sootily, hauling old-style carriages with slam doors and individual compartments. What is it about the Dublin trains of that era? They seemed to inspire stories of a salacious nature. This was the case when J.P. Donleavy's hero Sebastian Dangerfield, in the novel *The Ginger Man,* took the train south from Westland Row Station. He had just bought some liver, which he placed on the rack in the crowded compartment before sitting down. Suddenly a man loudly said, 'Sir, I say, there are ladies present in the carriage.' He noticed that people in the seat opposite were writhing and wriggling. A young lady blushed and pressed her book up to her face. Eventually, as he neared his stop, he looked down and realised that his fly was open and that he was on full display. Our hero grabs his blood-stained parcel of liver from the rack and, as he leaps out, there is a shout from behind: 'You can't remember your meat at all today.'

John Betjeman told a darker yarn in his novella, which was never published. In Betjeman's biography, the author Bevis Hillier recounts how this novella chronicles the travails of an aristocratic Standish O'Grady. In one episode, although a little geographically challenged (Broadstone Station and Westland Row are not directly connected by the loop line), it tells of the camp O'Grady informing his sister of an official letter he has just received: 'It is a warrant for my arrest for being detected in unnatural vice on the loop line between Westland Row and the Broadstone Station on the 21st of August 1932.'

Betjeman had been appointed press secretary to the British Legation in neutral Dublin in 1941, during what is known euphemistically in Ireland as the 'Emergency' (during the Second World War). He knew Dublin and Ireland well, having made many trips over the previous decades to visit his friends, who were mainly of the Anglo-Irish Ascendancy (the Dublin writer Brendan Behan acidly defined an Anglo-Irishman as a 'Protestant with a horse').

Dublin, with its exquisite Georgian and Victorian architecture, was a virtual playground for Betjeman and he enjoyed inspecting the nooks and crannies of the city. Novellas touching on vice were not his only interest – he had a particular affection for churches. The fine Monkstown Church to the south of Dublin, dating from 1831 to a design by John Semple, is reputed to have been his favourite in the city. Travel there to observe the Gothic castellations, like pieces on a chess board; look at the unusual and eccentric plaster decoration within and one can see why Betjeman came here. It is one of the most flamboyant interiors of any 19th-century building in the Dublin area.

Betjeman's duties as a press attaché were not onerous. Due to a shortage of newsprint, the Irish newspapers did not have much space for anodyne press releases, so he could concentrate on socialising with the eccentric mix of aristocrats, poets and writers that made up wartime Dublin society. Surprisingly, there was some socialising with diplomats in the Axis embassies. Mr Ishihashi, the Japanese press attaché, was dubbed Mr 'Itchy-Scratchy' by Betjeman. There has been much speculation that Betjeman's duties in Dublin extended to a touch of spying. If he was indeed spying, his effectiveness was open to question. This poet and aesthete was no James Bond.

Amid the constant round of parties in the city, alcohol and gossip flowed freely. One party held in a house in a southern suburb proved to be memorable. It was gate-crashed by one Francis Macnamara, father-in-law of the Welsh writer Dylan Thomas. Macnamara was well lubricated and became noisily obnoxious. Betjeman and a fellow guest at the party, an American journalist, grappled with the interloper and succeeded in ejecting him into the garden, after which they locked the door. The party continued without incident and Betjeman stayed overnight. There was much shock the next morning when it was discovered in the garden that carved into the lawn was a massive swastika. Betjeman hurriedly helped the host to retrieve the discarded turf and reinstate the lawn to its former pristine state, in the bourgeois heart of neutral Dublin.

HODDY, MONTO AND THE WANKEL ENGINE
1958

In the 1970s, the Buttery in Trinity College Dublin was an atmospheric cellar where students lurked and confirmed their general reputation as layabouts. As well as drinks, here was food of the calorific kind (burgers, chips and, on occasion, overcooked vegetables). At one table sat the local Trotskyites. Was that the scruffily dressed Republican Club types over there, planning the socialist republic? The braying sound came from the table held by the Rowing Club, loud and with public-school syllables. And who was that elderly man, wearing denim jeans and jacket, newspaper under his arm, moving between the tables? Why, it was George Desmond Hodnett, jazz critic of the *Irish Times*.

Hoddy, as he was affectionately known, was a habitué of Trinity College and the Buttery, and a legend in his own lunchtime (sadly, he died in 1990). It was vaguely known that he had studied law at Trinity. Popular among students was the story that he had given tutorials in law to the American Gainor Crist (on whom J.P. Donleavy had based the hero of his novel *The Ginger Man*). Crist was reputed to have frequently paused the tutorials while he proceeded to, shall we say, sojourn with his girlfriend, all in the same Trinity room. It was said that Hoddy claimed to have invented many things, including the Wankel rotary engine (which might have raised the eyebrows of German engineer Felix Wankel).

Wankel engine or not, Hoddy was a well-known songwriter. In 1958 he rattled off a song for a revue. This bawdy composition, with a rousing chorus, was picked up by Luke Kelly of the Dubliners, who sang it at a concert. The surprising thing is, this tale of boisterous carousing by the high and mighty in low places became one of the folk group's most popular songs. 'Monto' has since become a perennial at most Irish social gatherings and is usually belted out late at night, all the sweeter when the singer has had a pint or five.

If all the verses were set down, to understand them one would need a large dictionary of Dublin slang. To give a flavour we will look at one verse and the chorus (to explain: the police/polis HQ/depot is in the Phoenix Park):

> Now when the Tsar of Russia and the King of Prussia
> Landed in the Phoenix Park in a big balloon,
> They asked the polis band to play 'The Wearin' of the Green'
> But the buggers in the depot didn't know the tune.
> So they both went up to Monto, Monto, Monto,
> Take her up to Monto, langeroo,
> To you!

More explanation: 'langeroo' is in a high state of inebriation, and 'Monto' was Montgomery Street. The street is now respectably renamed as Foley Street, after the eminent 19th-century sculptor, John Henry Foley (see page 48).

Hoddy got it right: Monto definitely needed to be celebrated in song. Over a century ago it was at the heart of a red-light district in Dublin's north inner city, much frequented by the soldiery. It was a busy spot – Dublin had a higher rate of prostitution than most comparable British cities in those years. Its poor reputation for vice and the perils arising spread far and wide. The dangers of the city's demi-monde drove one correspondent to write in the days of the Raj: '… the worst possible news which can reach those interested in the moral welfare of the military in India is that a regiment has been ordered to Dublin … Dublin holds absolutely the lowest reputation amongst the cities of the homeland as a contaminating centre.'

BONO MUSIC: HIGH NOTES AND TARNISHED SAINTS

1960

Have you ever wondered how rock god Bono got his name? Paul David Hewson (born 1960) and his friends met at Mount Temple School in north Dublin and in 1976 formed a group. There was a hearing-aid store called Bonavox in central Dublin, and Bona Vox in Latin means 'good voice'. 'Bono' was taken from that appellation – and what better name could there be for the young Hewson?

The group U2, with their great music and meaningful lyrics, struck a chord. They enjoyed a stellar rise during the 1980s and produced superb albums like *The Joshua Tree*. Over the next decade they are in danger of being the next generation to follow the Rolling Stones as the (still lively) Grand Old Men of Rock'n'Roll.

Bono and his fellow band members have made the transition from a Dublin northside upbringing to being fabulously rich very well. He himself lives in Killiney, an affluent southern suburb of Dublin. With fellow band member the Edge, he invested in an iconic hotel in central Dublin, the Art-Deco Clarence, and refurbished it to full glory. The group celebrated their association with the hotel by belting out their tunes to *le tout* Dublin. They did this from on high, on the balcony of the newly added penthouse (which has all amenities, including baby grand piano and outdoor hot tub).

'Bono's Facebook stake to make him the richest rocker on earth' was the headline on MTV in 2012. He was far-sighted enough to invest in a substantial chunk of Facebook as a start-up company. Even after the subsequent drop in share value of Facebook following its stock-market launch, it is estimated that he made more out of this investment than he ever did from his day job as rock star.

With his characteristic all-enveloping sunglasses, the singer has over the years immersed himself in humanitarian work. He and the group have played many charity and aid concerts. Bono has immediate entrée to world leaders in his mission to help Africa and other poor parts of the globe. The Dublin lead singer was well on the way to acquiring the persona of a latter-day saint. Mother Teresa or Albert Schweitzer, anyone? However, life on the pedestal can be dangerous, with the ever-present danger of a fall.

Trouble was brewing: in an unexpected move, U2 Inc. had decided to move part of their business affairs to the Netherlands in 2006, after a cap was placed on tax breaks for artists in Ireland. All very proper and legal, said the U2 management company: U2 gains its income from around the world and pays taxes accordingly.

Nevertheless, some fans thought it was peculiar and that the saintly persona had become a little tarnished. In 2011 there was a flurry at a keynote performance by U2 at Glastonbury. A protest group erected a 20-foot balloon emblazoned with 'U pay your taxes 2'. One commentator said, 'Bono's attitude to what tax is all about is ill thought out. Tax is about citizenship.' Meanwhile, the group's native country, Ireland − following the global crisis − is in a financial mess and has had to be bailed out. Tax revenue is at a premium, with cutbacks in all government expenditure, including hospitals and schools, and a little more of Bono's massive wealth would surely come in handy.

GROTESQUE, UNBELIEVABLE, BIZARRE AND UNPRECEDENTED

1982

Here is a tragic tale, which merges into farce. It starts with one Malcolm MacArthur, an eccentric and flamboyant character who mixed with the cream of Dublin society, including some of its leading lawyers. Born in 1946, he came from a wealthy farming family and was well educated. But MacArthur had no job and by 1982 he was running out of money, having spent his generous inheritance. He decided to rob a bank and devised a plan, which he set in place in a methodical manner. To disguise himself he grew a beard and acquired a hat and spectacles. For a robbery he would need a gun and took note of a newspaper advertisement by a farmer for a shotgun for sale.

Next, he needed a car. One hot and sunny evening, he went to the large green expanse on the outskirts of Dublin, the Phoenix Park. There, he spotted a small car. It was owned by a nurse, Bridie Gargan, who was sunbathing in the park on her day off. MacArthur forced her to the car and bludgeoned her with a lump hammer. As he drove through the city streets with the dying nurse in the back seat, a passing ambulance driver noticed the nursing sticker on the car. The driver assumed it was a doctor, with an injured patient, who was trying to get to hospital. He switched on the siren and escorted the car towards the nearest hospital. MacArthur managed to divert within the hospital grounds and make his escape.

The next chapter in this saddening tale came three days later when MacArthur made his way to meet the farmer who was selling the shotgun. A sale did not take place. Instead, the farmer's body was found in a bog the next day, killed by a shotgun blast. In an unprecedented outbreak of murder and mayhem in Ireland, a great hue and cry ensued. The Garda Síochána issued a description of the suspect and began a massive manhunt.

Several weeks later MacArthur was apprehended. He was found staying at an apartment in Dalkey, to the south of Dublin, belonging to one Patrick Connolly. The extraordinary thing was that Connolly was the Attorney General of the Irish Government, the highest law officer in the land. As it turns out, he was unaware that his house guest, MacArthur, a social acquaintance, was a killer on the run. Equally incredibly, it transpired that Connolly had, a few days before, attended with MacArthur a football match at Croke Park in Dublin, driven there in his state car by its police driver. MacArthur watched the match from the stands while Connolly was in a VIP box where, by coincidence, the Garda Commissioner was also in attendance. After the discovery of MacArthur at his apartment, Connolly, strangely unaware of the public furore that was to ensue, proceeded to the United States for a holiday, planned well in advance of the recent incident. However, events followed the Attorney General. The day after his arrival in New York the *New York Post* carried the headline: 'Irish Biggie flees here after slay scandal'. That afternoon, Connolly flew back to London on Concorde and then back to Dublin. He resigned his office the next day.

As might be imagined, there was a stunned reaction across the country. The scandal rocked the government of the Taoiseach Charles Haughey, himself a controversial politician. Rattled and defensive, Haughey told the media that it was 'a bizarre happening, an unprecedented situation, a grotesque situation, an almost unbelievable mischance'. A prominent critic of Haughey dubbed this the GUBU affair (Grotesque, Unbelievable, Bizarre and Unprecedented), an epithet that dogged Haughey for the rest of his colourful career. MacArthur was duly convicted of murder in a Dublin court and is expected to be permanently released by the time you read this.

STATUESQUE LADIES, CEAUSESCU AND RYANAIR

1985

Warning: before you read this piece, you have to pay a service charge of £5. Please put it in the post to the publisher. Please also click here, that you have read and agreed to the terms and conditions.

As you drive through the jumble of buildings that make up the Dublin Airport complex, you pass the sign for the mortuary building. Just past this memento mori you can see, to the left, an undistinguished low-rise office block. This is the headquarters of Europe's largest budget airline, Ryanair. Within these confines there may be folks planning more additions to the gaiety of nations, such as new kinds of scratch cards, more boxes to untick on a labyrinthine internet booking page and much, much more. Here is the centre of it all, where a multitude of new hubs are being planned for obscure airports that, by a miracle of geography and imagination, have been renamed the same as large cities 80 miles away. Is there a padded cell here, one wonders, where staff can go to de-stress from the toil of thinking up new ways to part the passenger from his or her money?

How did this great high-flying empire start off? Modestly is the brief answer. With a share capital of £1 and 25 staff, it opened as a short-haul airline in 1985, operating turboprops from Waterford in the southeast of Ireland to London Gatwick. Next came a great leap forward in 1987 when it did a deal to 'wet lease' a fleet of BAC 1-11 planes (that is, they came with a pilot and engineers). These were a twin-jet British design manufactured under licence in Romania, then under Ceausescu's rule. The flight attendants were Irish, but the pilots were Romanian. All flight announcements were made (in English) by the flight attendants, the pilots confining their communications to those with Major Tom in ground control. The only clue that the planes came courtesy of Mr Ceauçescu was the signs advising of the location of the life-jacket, in English and Romanian.

It was a seminal event when Michael O'Leary joined the company. His visit to Southwest Airlines in the US proved to be an inspiration – he adopted its pioneering low-cost, no-frills approach. In turn, European aviation was being deregulated and the behemoth national airlines were now being exposed to competition for the first time. O'Leary negotiated a cracking deal with Boeing in 2001, right at the time of a collapse in demand for their planes, purchasing 125 new Boeing 737-800s at a deep discount. This acquisition of a fleet of new efficient planes has been one of the fundamentals of Ryanair's success ever since. Extract money from the passenger, yet overall offer a low ticket price, keep costs to a minimum, hedge one's aviation fuel here and there. All of these have been key for Ryanair to generate stellar profits in an industry known for its losses.

The rise and rise of the share price has made O'Leary a rich man. He is willing to speak his mind. Don't get him started about the European Union! Another perennial battle is with Dublin Airport around its monopoly and their landing charges. On one occasion there was a radio news report about an issue that involved the then Irish Minister for Transport, Mary O'Rourke, an endearing lady. When subsequently interviewed, she happened to mention that she was taking a bath in her Dublin apartment when she heard the particular radio report. Ryanair responded with a full-page advertisement showing an eye-catching cartoon of the minister reclining in her bath, with the caption: 'Mary, Mary, quite contrary. How does your monopoly grow?'

All publicity is good publicity. Many of the cabin staff are statuesque Eastern Europeans. The airline had the wonderful wheeze of doing a Pirelli calendar facsimile: 12 months of flight attendants in some déshabillé, in the Cabin Crew Calendar – all for charity, dontcha know!

Finally, we have the strange tale of applying Ryanair rules to the road. Currently on the airline, if you want to avoid the interminable queues, pay £5 to get priority boarding, then you can sail past the heaving plebs. O'Leary has a practical turn of mind and applied the same priority to getting himself around town quickly. In Dublin taxis are allowed to use bus lanes, thus avoiding the equally interminable queues. O'Leary bought himself a taxi licence, and now his driver can take him at some speed through Dublin and onwards to his large estate near Mullingar in the Irish midlands.

THE GENERAL AND
THE OLD MASTERS
1986

During the 1980s a Dublin criminal, one Martin Cahill, sprang to prominence. Brought up in a working-class area, he took to crime at an early age and in his teenage years was soon sent away to a reform school on being convicted for burglary. Later, he was rehoused in a council house in the southern suburb of Rathmines. Cahill never worked and signed on for the dole, but managed to own expensive properties. He was short, stocky and balding, with an unprepossessing demeanour. Despite having little schooling he was an excellent planner and meticulous in the execution of his crimes. His gang carried off a notorious run of robberies, including a daring heist of around £2m worth of jewels in 1983.

Cahill, now dubbed the 'General', pulled off a 'spectacular' when he robbed Russborough House in 1986. This was the home of the elderly millionaire Sir Alfred Beit, who had amassed a collection of outstanding Old Masters (in 1974, the IRA had stolen these paintings, which were soon recovered). The General struck one night and made off with a selection of the finest paintings, including Vermeer's 'Lady Writing a Letter with Her Maid'. It proved impossible to fence such a well-known collection of paintings and, eventually, most of these were recovered. Many are now in the keeping of the National Gallery of Ireland in Merrion Square in Dublin, where they are on (safe!) display to the public.

The General established a reputation for ruthlessness. One of his associates, whom he suspected of cheating him, was captured and nailed to the floor by his hands and feet. He placed a bomb under the car of the Irish government's chief forensic scientist, severely injuring him. The Garda Síochána set up a special surveillance unit to take a close interest in the criminal. He was under continuous watch and unmarked police cars were a permanent feature outside his home.

The General now enjoyed notoriety. His bizarre doings became a feature in the press and were a staple of television current affairs programmes. Undeterred by the publicity, he took to walking the Dublin streets, permanently wearing a hood. In one court appearance, he dropped his trousers to reveal his shorts, emblazoned with pictures of Mickey Mouse. His domestic arrangements were also unusual. He had two separate families: he was married to one lady, but also lived for part of the time in another house with her sister.

However, time was running out for the General and his peculiar existence. On 18 August 1994, as part of his regular routine, he drove from one of his houses to return some videos to a video store. He headed down Oxford Road in Ranelagh and slowed at a T-junction. There, a masked man stepped out and calmly shot Martin Cahill dead with a .357 Magnum revolver, then hopped on the back of an associate's motorcycle and sped away. At the funeral one of the family wreaths on Cahill's coffin read 'Que sera sera'.

There has been speculation as to who was responsible. One theory was that it was the IRA who ordered the hit, tired of this insolent criminal with alleged ties to the northern loyalist paramilitary group, the UDA. Another is that the motive was down to friction between the General and other Dublin criminals.

The curious life and times of the General have been portrayed on film and TV. Notable among the films is *The General*, with Brendan Gleeson, directed by John Boorman (1998), which won the best film award at Cannes. Another picture loosely based around Cahill's life was the 'crime-caper comedy' *Ordinary Decent Criminal* (2000) with Kevin Spacey and a host of other Hollywood stars.

DUBLIN SIGHTS:
WRY FLOWS THE LIFFEY
1988

What follows is neither for the faint of heart nor the politically correct. Young readers, please avert your eyes, turn away and put this book down. For now we look at the strange (or appalling? – you decide!) custom of Dubliners to refer to various worthy sights, statues and installations in the city using juvenile, disrespectful, even scatological terms. The grander it is, the wryer the comment.

For example, there is a fine statue that was commissioned by a civic-minded and wealthy benefactor at great cost in 1988. It was placed in the centre of O'Connell Street, the principal thoroughfare. There she sat, Anna Livia, personifying the river in Dublin. A fountain flowed and the waters that surged along by the statue represented the passage of the River Liffey as it flowed from the mountains to the wider reaches of Dublin Bay. However, the citizenry were having none of this; they did not appreciate the aesthetic. They dubbed it 'the Floozie in the Jacuzzi'; 'Anna Rexia'; 'Viagra Falls'; 'Bidet Mulligan'; and, steel yourself, dear reader: 'The hoor in the sewer' ('hoor' being colloquial for whore). In time the city council realised that there was not any great appreciation for the statue and it now languishes in a pleasant little (obscure) park to the West of the city centre.

And the lèse majesté doesn't stop there. What about the rather nice set of figures in bronze by the Ha'penny Bridge that shows two ladies chatting, with their shopping bags resting on the ground? To the populace this was the 'hags with the bags'. The fine statue of Oscar Wilde lounging on a rock in Merrion Square, sporting an enigmatic smile, is 'the queer with the leer' or the 'fag on a crag'.

141

Go to College Green, in the lee of Trinity College. Here you see the figure of a young lady with a large décolleté. This depicts Molly Malone (from the song 'Cockles and Mussels' – 'she wheeled her wheelbarrow through streets broad and narrow'). It is variously known as the 'tart with the cart'; 'the dolly with the trolley'; 'the trollop with the scallop' or 'the dish with the fish'.

There's more: the Luas light rail system that weaves its way through the impeccably affluent south suburbs is known as 'the choo-choo for the too-few'. James Connolly, the great labour leader, is commemorated with his own statue. Behind this is portrayed in bronze the banner of the socialist Irish Citizen Army, 'The Plough and the Stars'. The tableau has been labelled 'the agitator with the rotivator'. Even poor James Joyce, natty with his walking stick at North Earl Street, has not escaped. He has been christened as 'the prick with the stick'.

MICHAEL COLLINS AND CAPTAIN AHAB
1996

Dublin is a cinematic city, with everything to add to the dramatic moment, from fine vistas to narrow atmospheric streets. Many movies have been filmed there. The 2011 film *Albert Nobbs* with Glenn Close was based in late 19th-century Dublin and filmed in the city. In 1979 Sean Connery featured in *The First Great Train Robbery*, filmed on location at Heuston railway station. *Educating Rita* (1983) with Michael Caine and Julie Walters was shot at Trinity College and Pearse railway station. Dublin has its dark, run-down and gritty areas too and these were put to good use in 1965 to depict East Berlin in *The Spy Who Came in from the Cold* with Richard Burton.

Perhaps the film that made the greatest impact in Dublin though was the 1996 movie *Michael Collins* with Liam Neeson, Alan Rickman and Julia Roberts. Much of the story of Collins (leader in the Irish War of Independence, 1917–21, then Commander-in-Chief of the Free State Army shot in an ambush in his native West Cork in 1922) had taken place in Dublin and this was reflected in the use of original locations around the city. The production was meticulously planned by the director, Neil Jordan, who was educated in Dublin and now lives south of the city. Among the many locations, Kilmainham Gaol was used to depict the prison camp where Collins was interned at Frongoch in North Wales. Incidentally, Kilmainham has also been used for scenes in the films *In the Name of the Father* and *The Italian Job*.

Dublin Castle featured in the scene where Collins took it over from the British, who were evacuating their positions and leaving Ireland. In line with the attention to detail, traffic lights on the adjacent Dame Street entrance were removed and rubber cobblestone mats laid on the Tarmac roadway. The Collins' movie was filmed in many parts of Dublin but the biggest effort was made in creating a massive set in a run-down area in the North of the city. It cost around £1.5m and took several months to erect, located in the grounds of St Brendan's Hospital, Grangegorman, which had once been a lunatic asylum. The set was a life-size facsimile of the General Post Office (GPO), set in Sackville (now O'Connell) Street. It featured burned-out trams and wrecked shops, all with the intent of showing the action around the GPO, centre of the 1916 Easter Rising, in which Collins had played a significant part. Other prominent buildings were also mocked-up there for the film.

The surprising thing is that such a meticulously crafted movie, with a well-known cast, was a financial disaster. Why was that? Firstly, Neil Jordan had been allowed to make the film by the Hollywood movie executive David Geffen because he was 'hot', having just made the successful psychological thriller *The Crying Game*. Perhaps there were flaws in the structure and screenplay. Jordan wrote the script for the Collins' film himself, a potentially dangerous thing for a director. At the opening, Collins is shown fighting in the GPO – there is no explanation given of who he is, where he comes from or what is driving him, the main protagonist. One cannot rewrite history but you can select parts of the subject's life to create the correct dramatic structure. One script doctor commented on this structure (where Collins is shown directing a guerrilla war, signing a treaty with the enemy; a split occurs between those pro and anti the treaty and he is killed by the anti-treaty side), comparing it with *Moby Dick*, arguing that it's as if Captain Ahab meets the whale, says 'Let's make a deal' and is then shot by a crew member. Probably the most brutal fact is that movie-goers in the US didn't know who Collins was and didn't care. While *Michael Collins* was an outstanding box-office success in Ireland, and won the Golden Lion for Best Film at the Venice Film Festival, it bombed in the important US market, and overall made a loss.

BLING, ITS AFTERMATH AND
THE LARGEST BANKING
LOSS IN HISTORY
2005

This is an outlandish tale of hubris and rapid decline. In its heyday around 2005, the Celtic Tiger (as the Irish economy has been dubbed) looked like a sleek feline, in comparison to the moth-eaten and mangy moggy it is today. An unprecedented wave of affluence swept Dublin. Skyscrapers parted the heavens, celestial knitting needles of prosperity. There was building everywhere, apartment blocks and offices. The motto was: fill every available plot of land with a building. Property developers were the new High Kings and all day long the airspace over Dublin resounded with the clatter of their chariot of choice, the helicopter. Down on the ground, travel was by Mercedes or, increasingly, luxury marques like the Bentley. In the affluent suburbs visible monuments to bling were created, as the developers demolished 19th-century homes and rebuilt them with the requisite helicopter pad. Banks were booming, lending vast sums of money to fuel this development. House prices rose and rose. When the common man could not afford to buy in Ireland any more, he looked abroad, to sate the essential Irish wish to acquire land (is it a folk-memory inherited from the days of the Famine and being tenants of the great landlords?). Even Dublin taxi drivers bought their apartment in Turkey or Bulgaria.

And then, Lehman Brothers crashed. The reverberations of this catastrophe soon burst the latter-day South Sea Bubble of the Irish property boom. The crash was precipitous. House and land prices plummeted. The inflated construction industry was left with nothing to build, and architects and lawyers went on the dole. The Polish builders returned home. Many skilled tradesmen emigrated,

some to build the Olympic Park in London. Government revenues dried up. And now, in the aftermath of the party, austerity is all and the Government will struggle for many years to plug the overspending gap, by cutting costs and interminably raising taxes.

Many countries overindulge or manage their economies badly and then suffer the consequences. What makes the Irish crash so different from others was the size of the development boom and its effect on the Irish financial system, in relation to what is a small country and economy. The property developers had borrowed huge sums from the banks. When the crash came, the developers went bankrupt and the banks, in turn, were left with enormous bad debts. On the night of 29 September 2008, the Irish Government, fearful of a run on the banks, stepped in and guaranteed all the Irish banks. Unwittingly, they were now committing the Irish taxpayer to be responsible for one of the biggest financial black holes ever.

Soon afterwards, the details began to emerge. The Irish banks owed £50bn to private bondholders. The European Central Bank (ECB) insisted that the Irish taxpayer had to pay all of this debt to the bondholders, if there was going to be a loan issued to bail out the Irish state. The ECB is run by bankers, so the principle applied is one of socialist banking: if a bank makes profits, bonuses all around; if the bank makes losses, then socialise the debts. Currently all of this is to be paid by the Irish taxpayer, who did not take out these loans. Just to put this burden in perspective, to compare on a pro-rata basis by population, in Britain this would amount to around £700bn.

And so, monuments to failed Mammon abound around Dublin. In the outer suburbs, there are ghost estates with decaying half-finished houses. Partly-built office blocks with weeds growing around dot the city. Many are now owned by the National Asset Management Agency, set up by the government to take the toxic assets of the banks under its wing. The banks had received these as collateral from the developers and they were now practically worthless.

The most curious and visible testimony to this sorry débâcle is the white concrete hulk that currently sits unfinished on North Wall Quay in Dublin. This was the proposed grandiose headquarters of the Anglo-Irish Bank. It was little more than a boutique bank, with a speciality of lending to property developers, and was at the centre of

a golden circle of the highest-flying (and not just in helicopters!) speculators. As the steel reinforcing bars rust in the salty Dublin docklands air, it's a poignant reminder of a world record, although not one to be proud of. The record is the biggest bank loss, for such a size of bank, in the history of banking: it was achieved by the Anglo-Irish Bank. This small bank, with only a handful of retail branches, managed to attain a loss of £24bn.

RAPIDLY GOING DOWN THE LIFFEY?
2013

Although over the centuries Dublin was looked upon by many of the native Irish as an alien city, in fact it has played a major role in Ireland's story for well over a thousand years. In 1988 Dublin Corporation, as it was then known, even organised a millennium year of celebrations, although there was very little specific evidence of much having happened in Dublin in 988.

The city's geographical location – halfway down the east coast of Ireland – meant that all major roads led to Dublin. This has continued so that today the motorway and rail systems all radiate from the capital. The result is that people from all parts of Ireland now live in Dublin, and the 'true blue Dub' of more than four or five generations is a rare bird indeed. Parts of the city, such as Rathmines and Drumcondra, were famous as places where young people coming up from the country would find accommodation when starting their first job. Also, many young people flooded out through the ports of Dublin and Dún Laoghaire en route to Liverpool and Holyhead, and often onwards by sea or train from there.

In recent decades various strange experiments were made by some governments, who shall remain nameless, to organise 'decentralisation' from Dublin. But whereas in other countries the idea was to devolve power to local administrations, in the weird logic of these proposals, power was to remain jealously guarded by the central administration: the Irish definition of 'decentralisation' meant the carving up of the national cake and scattering it for the benefit of a certain political party all around the country. This was not on the grounds of any national regional or spatial strategy, but so as to bolster political support and allow party members with large land holdings to benefit from inflated prices for land for government offices and housing for those unfortunates who had to migrate from the capital to the remotest parts of Ireland.

It was notable that Cork, the second city of Ireland, which has the benefit of an airport, train service, motorway, port and all the accoutrements of a large city, was not to be favoured by this policy. Could Cork's political leanings have had anything to do with this?

The story among the Dubs is that if a Corkonian comes to Dublin, they throw a stone in the Liffey, and if it floats, they go home again! In fact it was often the brightest from the rural areas (whom the Dubs called 'culchies', probably because of their agricultural roots) who came to Dublin and ran the country, much to the resentment of the resident 'jackeens' (so called because the rural dwellers associated them with John (or Jack) Bull).

But the influx of outsiders into the capital did not change the habits of generations: whereas English (as opposed to British) people abroad tended not to speak to each other, for reasons of class or stiff upper lip, Irish people always talked to each other, usually to find that they had a number of friends and acquaintances in common, unless they were actually related by a marriage that took place a century previously! Many of these relationships were forged in Dublin, where all roads led, and where there were much better options for education and employment.

Because of the country's disturbed history, many of the events upon which the fate of Ireland turned were played out in Dublin: the Vikings, Anglo-Normans (really Welsh-Normans) and English setting up shop, only to culminate in the Empire-shattering uprising of Easter 1916. This was the most ruinous of battles to be held in any European capital in centuries, and from those ruins the whole country, with one major exception, arose changed.

In 2016 Ireland will celebrate the centenary of those events in the strangest of circumstances: having fought for its independence over hundreds of years, and gained its sovereignty against all the odds, her leaders sold the country's freedom down the river, and the population now finds itself under the thumb of the International Monetary Fund, the European Union and the European Central Bank. The thousands of highly skilled Irish, other Europeans and people from around the world who live and work in the greater Dublin area have their lives dominated by large multinational firms attracted by the lower tax rates, but the shadow over it all is that of the Troika.

When St Patrick (after whom one of the two cathedrals in Dublin is named) preached about the Holy Trinity, it is said that he used the symbol of the shamrock to indicate that there were three persons in the one God. Ireland, after one of the world's greatest parties in honour of the god of economic folly, has now progressed to having three lenders in one Troika, now indicated by Dublin's traditional symbol of three brass balls over the pawnbroker's shop.

BIBLIOGRAPHY

Bardon, J., *A History of Ireland* (Gill and Macmillan, Dublin, 2009)

Barry, M., *50 Things to Do in Dublin* (DMCRS, Dublin, 2012)

Barry, M., *Victorian Dublin Revealed* (Andalus Press, Dublin, 2011)

Barry, M., *Tales of the Permanent Way* (Andalus Press, Dublin, 2009)

Bolger, M., Dublin: *City of Literature*, (O'Brien Press, Dublin, 2011)

Casey, C., *Dublin* (Yale University Press, New Haven and London, 2005)

Connolly, C., *Michael Collins* (Weidenfeld and Nicolson, London, 1996)

Connolly, S.J., Ed., *The Oxford Companion to Irish History* (Oxford University Press, Oxford, 1998)

Coogan, T.P., *De Valera* (Hutchinson, London, 1993)

Cullen, L.M., *Princes & Pirates* (Dublin Chamber of Commerce, Dublin, 1983)

Ekin, D., *The Stolen Village* (O'Brien Press, Dublin, 2008)

Gillis, L., *The Fall of Dublin* (Mercier Press, Cork, 2011)

Hart, M., *The Irish Game* (Plume, New York, 2004)

Hillier, B., *John Betjeman, the Biography* (John Murray, London, 2007)

Holmes, R., *Wellington, the Iron Duke*, (HarperCollins, London, 2003)

Joyce, J., Murtagh, P., *The Boss* (Poolbeg, Dublin, 1997)

Keay, J., *The Great Arc* (HarperCollins, London, 2001)

Lalor, B., Ed., *The Encyclopaedia of Ireland* (Yale University Press, New Haven and London, 2003)

Lalor, B., *Ultimate Dublin Guide* (O'Brien Press, Dublin, 1991)

Liddy, P., *Dublin be Proud* (Chadworth, Dublin, 1987)

MacLoughlin, A., *Guide to Historic Dublin* (Gill and Macmillan, Dublin, 1979)

Malcolmson, A.P.W., *The Pursuit of the Heiress* (Ulster Historical Foundation, 2006)

Marshall, D., *The Life and Times of Victoria* (Weidenfeld and Nicolson, London, 1972)

McGuire, V., *Roddy Connolly and the Struggle for Socialism in Ireland* (Cork University Press, Cork, 2008)

McNamara, M., Mooney, P., *Women in Parliament: Ireland 1918–2000* (Wolfhound Press, Dublin, 2000)

Mulvihill, M., *Ingenious Ireland* (TownHouse, Dublin, 2002)

Nicholson, R., *The Ulysses Guide* (New Island, Dublin, 2002)

O'Brien, J.V., *Dear Dirty Dublin: A City in Distress, 1899–1916* (University of California Press, Berkeley, 1982)

O'Connor, U., *Oliver St John Gogarty, A Poet and His Times* (O'Brien Press, Dublin, 2000)

O'Maitiú, S., *Dublin's Suburban Towns 1834–1930* (Four Courts Press, Dublin, 2003)

Pakenham, T. & V., *Dublin, a Traveller's Companion* (Constable, London, 1988)

Pierce, J., *The Unmasking of Oscar Wilde* (Ignatius Press, 2005)

Sammon, P., *Greenspeak – Ireland in Her Own Words* (TownHouse, Dublin, 2002)

Shepherd, E., Beesley, G., *Dublin & South Eastern Railway* (Midland Publishing Company, Leicester, 1998)

Showers, B.J., *Gothic Dublin* (Nonsuch, Dublin, 2006)

Vignoles, K.H., *Charles Blacker Vignoles: Romantic Engineer* (Cambridge University Press, Cambridge, 2010)

Woodham-Smith, C., *Queen Victoria* (Alfred A. Knopf, New York, 1972)